What You Should Know About Inflation

by HENRY HAZLITT

FUNK & WAGNALLS / NEW YORK

Preface

This book first appeared in 1960; a revised edition was published in 1965. For the present edition the main statistical comparisons and tables have been brought up to date. Where older figures and comparisons illustrate a principle or consequence fully as well as more recent figures would, however, they have been allowed to stand.

No book on inflation, in fact, can ever be completely up to date. New statistics on wholesale prices and consumer prices appear every month. New figures on the country's stock of money appear each week. On the organized commodity markets, prices are changing every day and every hour. And as long as inflation continues most of the changes are upward.

If I were to try to tell here what has happened since either the 1965 or the 1960 edition, I could do it in as little as three words: inflation has continued. Between the end of 1964 and the end of 1967 the nation's stock of paper money (currency plus demand bank deposits) was increased by $22 billion, or 12 per cent. Between the end of 1959 and the end of 1967 the nation's stock of paper money was increased by $40 billion, or 22 per cent. From the end of 1964 till the month of writing this the average of wholesale prices has increased 7 per cent. In the same period the cost of living has gone up 10 per cent. Since the end of 1959, it has gone up 17 per cent.

If we carry these comparisons still further back, we find that since 1939 the cost of living has gone up 145 per cent, which means that the dollar today will buy only as much as 41 cents bought then.

In other words, the inflation of the last thirty years has already wiped out about 60 per cent of the purchasing power of peoples' savings deposits, mortgages, bonds (including government bonds), life-insurance benefits, and fixed pensions. It has impoverished the poor and the elderly, and all those who are not financially sophisticated enough, or whose resources are not great enough, to know how to or even to be able to buy common stocks, or real estate, or paintings by famous artists, in order to protect themselves to some extent against the dwindling value of their dollars. Worse, in all those who are retired or too old or disabled to work, the prospect of a still further inflation has created a haunting fear of a further but unknown erosion in the buying power of their pensions or savings.

One grim irony is that the "War on Poverty," with its massive public spending and chronic deficits, has meant increased poverty for millions.

It is in any case impossible (as explained in Chapter 43) for everybody to protect himself against inflation. A minority can do so only at the expense of the rest of us. The only cure for the evils of inflation is to halt the inflation itself. Any government can do this if it has the will.

HENRY HAZLITT

May, 1968

Contents

1

What Inflation Is

No subject is so much discussed today—or so little understood—as inflation. The politicians in Washington talk of it as if it were some horrible visitation from without, over which they had no control—like a flood, a foreign invasion, or a plague. It is something they are always promising to "fight"—if Congress or the people will only give them the "weapons" or "a strong law" to do the job.

Yet the plain truth is that our political leaders have brought on inflation by their own money and fiscal policies. They are promising to fight with their right hand the conditions brought on with their left.

Inflation, always and everywhere, is primarily caused by an increase in the supply of money and credit. In fact, inflation *is* the increase in the supply of money and credit. If you turn to the American College Dictionary, for example, you will find the first definition of inflation given as follows: "Undue *expansion* or increase of the *currency* of a country, esp. by the issuing of paper money not redeemable in specie."

In recent years, however, the term has come to be used in a radically different sense. This is recognized in the second definition given by the American College Dictionary:

"A substantial *rise of prices* caused by an undue expansion in paper money or bank credit." Now obviously a rise of prices *caused* by an expansion of the money supply is not the same thing as the expansion of the money supply itself. A cause or condition is clearly not identical with one of its consequences. The use of the word "inflation" with these two quite different meanings leads to endless confusion.

The word "inflation" originally applied solely to the quantity of money. It meant that the volume of money was *inflated,* blown up, overextended. It is not mere pedantry to insist that the word should be used only in its original meaning. To use it to mean "a rise in prices" is to deflect attention away from the real cause of inflation and the real cure for it.

Let us see what happens under inflation, and why it happens. When the supply of money is increased, people have more money to offer for goods. If the supply of goods does not increase—or does not increase as much as the supply of money—then the prices of goods will go up. Each individual dollar becomes less valuable because there are more dollars. Therefore more of them will be offered against, say, a pair of shoes or a hundred bushels of wheat than before. A "price" is an *exchange ratio* between a dollar and a unit of goods. When people have more dollars, they value each dollar less. Goods then rise in price, not because goods are scarcer than before, but because dollars are more abundant.

In the old days, governments inflated by clipping and debasing the coinage. Then they found they could inflate cheaper and faster simply by grinding out paper money on a printing press. This is what happened with the French assignats in 1789, and with our own currency during the Revolutionary War. Today the method is a little more indirect. Our government sells its bonds or other IOU's to the banks. In payment, the banks create "deposits" on their books against which the government can draw. A bank in turn may sell its government IOU's to the Federal Reserve Bank, which pays for them either by creating a deposit credit or having more Federal Reserve notes printed and paying them out. This is how money is manufactured.

The greater part of the "money supply" of this country is represented not by hand-to-hand currency but by bank deposits which are drawn against by checks. Hence when most economists measure our money supply they add demand deposits (and now frequently, also, time deposits) to currency outside of banks to get the total. The total of money and credit, including commercial time deposits, was $51 billion at the end of 1939 and $365 billion at the end of 1967. This increase of 612 per cent in the supply of money was overwhelmingly the reason why wholesale prices rose 153 per cent in the same period.

2

Some Qualifications

It is often argued that to attribute inflation solely to an increase in the volume of money is "oversimplification." This is true. Many qualifications have to be kept in mind.

For example, the "money supply" must be thought of as including not only the supply of hand-to-hand currency, but the supply of bank credit—especially in the United States, where most payments are made by check.

It is also an oversimplification to say that the value of an individual dollar depends simply on the *present* supply of dollars outstanding. It depends also on the *expected future* supply of dollars. If most people fear, for example, that the supply of dollars is going to be even greater a year from now than at present, then the present value of the dollar (as measured by its purchasing power) will be lower than the present quantity of dollars would otherwise warrant.

Again, the value of any monetary unit, such as the dollar, depends not merely on the *quantity* of dollars but on their *quality*. When a country goes off the gold standard, for example, it means in effect that gold, or the right to get gold, has suddenly turned into mere paper. The value of the monetary unit therefore usually falls immediately, even if there has not yet been any increase in the quantity of money. This is because the people have more faith in gold than they have in the promises or judgment of the government's monetary managers. There is hardly a case on record, in fact, in which departure from the gold standard has not soon been followed by a further increase in bank credit and in printing-press money.

In short, the value of money varies for basically the same reasons as the value of any commodity. Just as the value of a bushel of wheat depends not only on the total present supply of wheat but on the expected future supply and on the quality of the wheat, so the value of a dollar depends on a similar variety of considerations. The value of money, like the value of goods, is not determined by merely mechanical or physical relationships, but primarily by psychological factors which may often be complicated.

In dealing with the causes and cure of inflation, it is one thing to keep in mind real complications; it is quite another to be confused or misled by needless or nonexistent complications.

For example, it is frequently said that the value of the dollar depends not merely on the quantity of dollars but on their "velocity of circulation." Increased "velocity of circulation," however, is not a cause of a further fall in the value of the dollar; it is itself one of the consequences of the fear that the value of the dollar is going to fall (or, to put it the other way round, of the belief that the price of goods is going to rise). It is this belief that makes people more eager to exchange dollars for goods. The emphasis by some writers

5

on "velocity of circulation" is just another example of the error of substituting dubious mechanical for real psychological reasons.

Another blind alley: in answer to those who point out that inflation is primarily caused by an increase in money and credit, it is contended that the increase in commodity prices often occurs *before* the increase in the money supply. This is true. This is what happened immediately after the outbreak of war in Korea. Strategic raw materials began to go up in price on the fear that they were going to be scarce. Speculators and manufacturers began to buy them to hold for profit or protective inventories. *But to do this they had to borrow more money from the banks.* The rise in prices was accompanied by an equally marked rise in bank loans and deposits. From May 31, 1950, to May 30, 1951, the loans of the country's banks increased by $12 billion. If these increased loans had not been made, and new money (some $6 billion by the end of January 1951) had not been issued against the loans, the rise in prices could not have been sustained. The price rise was made possible, in short, only by an increased supply of money.

Some Popular Fallacies

One of the most stubborn fallacies about inflation is the assumption that it is caused, not by an increase in the quantity of money, but by a "shortage of goods."

It is true that a *rise in prices* (which, as we have seen, should not be identified with inflation) can be caused *either* by an increase in the quantity of money *or* by a shortage of goods—or partly by both. Wheat, for example, may rise in price either because there is an increase in the supply of money or a failure of the wheat crop. But we seldom find, even in conditions of total war, a *general* rise of prices caused by a *general* shortage of goods. Yet so stubborn is the fallacy that inflation is caused by a "shortage of goods," that even in the Germany of 1923, after prices had soared hundreds of billions of times, high officials and millions of Germans were blaming the whole thing on a general "shortage of goods"—at the very moment when foreigners were coming in and buying German goods with gold or their own currencies at prices lower than those of equivalent goods at home.

The rise of prices in the United States since 1939 is

constantly being attributed to a "shortage of goods." Yet official statistics show that our rate of industrial production in 1959 was 177 per cent higher than in 1939, or nearly three times as great. Nor is it any better explanation to say that the rise in prices in wartime is caused by a shortage in *civilian* goods. Even to the extent that civilian goods were really short in time of war, the shortage would not cause any substantial rise in prices if taxes took away as large a percentage of civilian income as rearmament took away of civilian goods.

This brings us to another source of confusion. People frequently talk as if a budget deficit were in itself both a necessary and a sufficient cause of inflation. A budget deficit, however, if fully financed by the sale of government bonds paid for out of real savings, need not cause inflation. And even a budget surplus, on the other hand, is not an assurance against inflation. This was shown in the fiscal year ended June 30, 1951, when there was substantial inflation *in spite of* a budget surplus of $3.5 billion. The same thing happened in spite of budget surpluses in the fiscal years 1956 and 1957. A budget deficit, in short, is inflationary only to the extent that it causes an increase in the money supply. And inflation can occur even with a budget surplus if there is an increase in the money supply notwithstanding.

The same chain of causation applies to all the so-called "inflationary pressures"—particularly the so-called "wage-price spiral." If it were not preceded, accompanied, or quickly followed by an increase in the supply of money, an increase in wages above the "equilibrium level" would not cause inflation; it would merely cause unemployment. And

8

an increase in prices without an increase of cash in people's pockets would merely cause a falling off in sales. Wage and price rises, in brief, are usually a *consequence* of inflation. They can *cause* it only to the extent that they force an increase in the money supply.

A Twenty-Year Record

I present in this chapter a chart comparing the increase in the cost of living, in wholesale commodity prices, and in the amount of bank deposits and currency, for the twenty-year period from the end of 1939 to the end of 1959.

Taking the end of 1939 as the base, and giving it a value of 100, the chart shows that in 1959 the cost of living (consumer prices) had increased 113 per cent over 1939, wholesale prices had increased 136 per cent, and the total supply of bank deposits and currency had increased 270 per cent.

The basic cause of the increase in wholesale and consumer prices was the increase in the supply of money and credit. There was no "shortage of goods." As we noticed in the preceding chapter, our rate of industrial production in the twenty-year period increased 177 per cent. But though the rate of industrial production almost tripled, the supply of money and credit almost quadrupled. If it had not been for the increase in production, the rise in prices would have been much greater than it actually was.

Nor, as we also saw in the last chapter, can the increase in prices be attributed to increased wage demands—to a "cost push." Such a theory reverses cause and effect. "Costs" are prices—prices of raw materials and services—and go up for the same reason as other prices do.

If we were to extend this chart to a total of 29 years—that is, to the end of 1967—it would show that, taking 1939 as a base, the cost of living increased 144 per cent, wholesale prices increased 153 per cent, and the total supply of bank deposits and currency increased 612 per cent in the period.

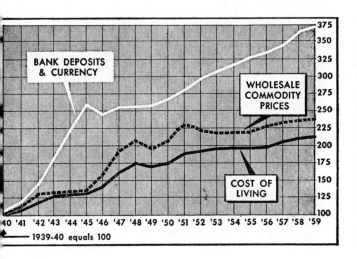

BANK DEPOSITS & CURRENCY

WHOLESALE COMMODITY PRICES

COST OF LIVING

'40 '41 '42 '43 '44 '45 '46 '47 '48 '49 '50 '51 '52 '53 '54 '55 '56 '57 '58 '59

1939-40 equals 100

5

False Remedy: Price Fixing

As long as we are plagued by false theories of what causes inflation, we will be plagued by false remedies. Those who ascribe inflation primarily to a "shortage of goods," for example, are fond of saying that "the answer to inflation is production." But this is at best a half-truth. It is impossible to bring prices down by increasing production if the money supply is being increased even faster.

The worst of all false remedies for inflation is price fixing and wage fixing. If more money is put into circulation, while prices are held down, most people will be left with unused cash balances seeking goods. The final result, barring a like increase in production, must be higher prices.

There are broadly two kinds of price fixing—"selective" and "over-all." With selective price fixing the government tries to hold down prices merely of a few strategic war materials or a few necessaries of life. But then the profit margin in producing these things becomes lower than the profit margin in producing other things, including luxuries. So "selective" price fixing quickly brings about a shortage of the very things whose production the government is most eager to encourage. Then bureaucrats turn to the specious idea of an over-all freeze. They talk (in the event of a war) of holding or returning to the prices and wages that existed on the day before war broke out. But the price level and the infinitely complex price and wage interrelationships of that day were the result of the state of supply and demand on that day. And supply and demand seldom remain the same, even for the same commodity, for two days running, even without major changes in the money supply.

It has been moderately estimated that there are some 9,000,000 different prices in the United States. On this basis we begin with more than 40 trillion *interrelationships* of these prices; and a change in one price always has repercussions on a whole network of other prices. The prices and price relationships on the day before the unexpected outbreak of a war, say, are presumably those roughly calculated to encourage a maximum balanced production of *peacetime* goods. They are obviously the wrong prices and price relationships to encourage the maximum production of *war* goods. Moreover, the price pattern of a given day always embodies many misjudgments and "inequities." No single mind, and no bureaucracy, has wisdom and knowledge enough to correct these. Every time a bureaucrat tries to correct one price or wage maladjustment or "inequity" he creates a score of new ones. And there is no precise standard that any two people seem able to agree on for measuring the economic "inequities" of a particular case.

Coercive price fixing would be an insoluble problem, in short, even if those in charge of it were the best-informed economists, statisticians, and businessmen in the country, and even if they acted with the most conscientious impartiality.

13

But they are subjected in fact to tremendous pressure by the organized pressure groups. Those in power soon find that price and wage control is a tremendous weapon with which to curry political favor or to punish opposition. That is why "parity" formulas are applied to farm prices and escalator clauses to wage rates, while industrial prices and dwelling rents are penalized.

Another evil of price control is that, although it is always put into effect in the name of an alleged "emergency," it creates powerful vested interests and habits of mind which prolong it or tend to make it permanent. Outstanding examples of this are rent control and exchange control. Price control is the major step toward a fully regimented or "planned" economy. It causes people to regard it as a matter of course that the government should intervene in every economic transaction.

But finally, and worst of all from the standpoint of inflation, price control diverts attention away from the only real cause of inflation—the increase in the quantity of money and credit. Hence it prolongs and intensifies the very inflation it was ostensibly designed to cure.

6

The Cure for Inflation

The cure for inflation, like most cures, consists chiefly in removal of the cause. The cause of inflation is the increase of money and credit. The cure is to stop increasing money and credit. The cure for inflation, in brief, is to stop inflating. It is as simple as that.

Although simple in principle, this cure often involves complex and disagreeable decisions on detail. Let us begin with the Federal budget. It is next to impossible to avoid inflation with a continuing heavy deficit. That deficit is almost certain to be financed by inflationary means—i.e., by directly or indirectly printing more money. Huge government expenditures are not in themselves inflationary—provided they are made wholly out of tax receipts, or out of borrowing paid for wholly out of real savings. But the difficulties in either of these methods of payment, once expenditures have passed a certain point, are so great that there is almost inevitably a resort to the printing press.

Moreover, although huge expenditures wholly met out of huge taxes are not necessarily *inflationary,* they inevitably reduce and disrupt production, and undermine any free enterprise system. The remedy for huge governmental expenditures is therefore not equally huge taxes, but a halt to reckless spending.

On the monetary side, the Treasury and the Federal Reserve System must stop creating artificially cheap money; i.e., they must stop arbitrarily holding down interest rates. The Federal Reserve must not return to the former policy of buying at par the government's own bonds. When interest rates are held artificially low, they encourage an increase in borrowing. This leads to an increase in the money and credit supply. The process works both ways—for it is necessary to increase the money and credit supply in order to keep interest rates artificially low. That is why a "cheap money" policy and a government-bond-support policy are simply two ways of describing the same thing. When the Federal Reserve Banks bought the government's $2\frac{1}{2}$ per cent bonds, say, at par, they held down the basic long-term interest rate to $2\frac{1}{2}$ per cent. And they paid for these bonds, in effect, by printing more money. This is what is known as "monetizing" the public debt. Inflation goes on as long as this goes on.

The Federal Reserve System, if it is determined to halt inflation and to live up to its responsibilities, will abstain from efforts to hold down interest rates and to monetize the public debt. It should return, in fact, to the tradition that the discount rate of the central bank should normally (and above all in an inflationary period) be a "penalty" rate—i.e., a rate higher than the member banks themselves get on their loans.

Congress should restore the required legal reserve ratio of the Federal Reserve Banks to the previous level of 35 and 40 per cent, instead of the level (even that abandoned) of 25 per cent put into effect as a war-inflation measure in June 1945. Later I shall discuss other means of preventing an undue increase in the supply of money and credit. But I should like to state here my conviction that the world will never work itself out of the present inflationary era until it returns to the gold standard. The gold standard provided a practically automatic check on internal credit expansion. That is why the bureaucrats abandoned it. In addition to its being a safeguard against inflation, it is the only system that has ever provided the world with the equivalent of an international currency.

The first question to be asked today is not *how* can we stop inflation, but do we really *want* to? For one of the effects of inflation is to bring about a redistribution of wealth and income. In its early stages (until it reaches the point where it grossly distorts and undermines production itself) it benefits some groups at the expense of others. The first groups acquire a vested interest in maintaining inflation. Too many of us continue under the delusion that we can beat the game—that we can increase our own incomes faster than our living costs. So there is a great deal of hypocrisy in the outcry against inflation. Many of us are shouting in effect: "Hold down everybody's price and income except my own."

Governments are the worst offenders in this hypocrisy. At the same time as they profess to be "fighting inflation" they follow a so-called "full employment" policy. As one advocate of inflation once put it in the *London Economist:* "Inflation is nine-tenths of *any* full employment policy."

What he forgot to add is that inflation must always end

in a crisis and a slump, and that worse than the slump itself may be the public delusion that the slump has been caused, not by the previous inflation, but by the inherent defects of "capitalism."

Inflation, to sum up, is the increase in the volume of money and bank credit in relation to the volume of goods. It is harmful because it depreciates the value of the monetary unit, raises everybody's cost of living, imposes what is in effect a tax on the poorest (without exemptions) at as high a rate as the tax on the richest, wipes out the value of past savings, discourages future savings, redistributes wealth and income wantonly, encourages and rewards speculation and gambling at the expense of thrift and work, undermines confidence in the justice of a free enterprise system, and corrupts public and private morals.

But it is never "inevitable." We can always stop it overnight, if we have the sincere will to do so.

7

Inflation Has Two Faces

It must be said, in sorrow, that the American public, generally speaking, not only does not understand the real cause and cure for inflation, but presents no united front against it. Feelings about inflation are confused and ambivalent. This is because inflation, like Janus, has two opposite faces. Whether we welcome or fear it depends upon the face we happen to look at. Or, putting the matter another way, we are each of us sometimes Dr. Jekyll and sometimes Mr. Hyde in our attitude toward inflation, depending upon how it seems to affect our personal interest at the moment.

All this was once vividly illustrated in a message to a special session of Congress, in 1947, by President Truman. "We already have an alarming degree of inflation," he declared; "and, even more alarming, it is getting worse." Yet he pointed with pride to the results of inflation at one moment and denounced them the next moment. He claimed credit for its popular consequences and blamed his political opponents for its unpopular consequences. Like the rest of us, the President wanted to have his shoes small on the outside and large on the inside.

It should be obvious that high prices, which everybody affects to deplore, and high money incomes, which everyone wants to achieve, are two sides of the same thing. Given the same amount of production, if you double the price level you double the national income. When President Truman boasted in July of 1947 that we had "surpassed previous high records" with a gross national product of $225 billion, he was boasting in large part of the higher dollar totals you get when you multiply volume of output by higher dollar prices.

At one point in his "anti-inflation" message Mr. Truman declared: "In terms of actual purchasing power, the average income of individuals after taxes has risen (since 1929) 39 per cent." But a little later he was asking, inconsistently, how "the cost of living can be brought and held in reasonable relationship to the incomes of the people." Yet if the incomes of the people had in fact already risen so much faster than living costs that the individual could buy nearly 40 per cent more goods than he could before, in what did the alleged inflation "emergency" of 1947 consist?

"Rents are rising," complained Mr. Truman at another point, "at the rate of about 1 per cent a month," and such a rise imposed an "intolerable strain" upon the family budget. But as the average weekly earnings of factory workers had then gone up 112 per cent since 1939, while rents had gone up only 9 per cent, the average worker paid, in fact, a far smaller percentage of his income for rent than he did before the war.

"The harsh effects of price inflation," said Mr. Truman at still another point, "are felt by wage earners, farmers, and businessmen." Clearly this did not refer to the inflation of their own prices, but of somebody else's. It is not the prices they got for their own goods and services, but the prices they had to pay for the goods and services of others, that they regarded as "harsh."

The real evil of inflation is that it redistributes wealth and income in a wanton fashion often unrelated to the contribution of different groups and individuals to production. All those who gain through inflation on net balance necessarily do so at the expense of others who lose through it on net balance. And it is often the biggest gainers by inflation who cry the loudest that they are its chief victims. Inflation is a twisted magnifying lens through which everything is confused, distorted, and out of focus, so that few men are any longer able to see realities in their true proportions.

8

What "Monetary Management" Means

Ever since the end of World War II, the public in nearly every country has been told that the gold standard is out-of-date, and what is needed in its place is "monetary management" by the experts. It is interesting to notice what some of the consequences of this have been.

When Sir Stafford Cripps, then Chancellor of the Exchequer, announced the devaluation of the British pound on September 18, 1949, Winston Churchill pointed out that Cripps had previously denied any such possibility no fewer than nine times. A United Press dispatch of September 18 listed nine such occasions. A haphazard search on my own part uncovered three more—on September 22 and 28, 1948, and April 30, 1949. Incorporating these in the UP list, we get the following record of denials:

Jan. 26, 1948—"No alteration in the value of sterling is contemplated by the British Government following the devaluation of the franc."

March 4, 1948—A reported plan to devalue the pound is "complete nonsense."

May 6, 1948—"The government has no intention of embarking on a program to devalue the pound."

Sept. 22, 1948—"There will be no devaluation of the pound sterling."

Sept. 28, 1948—The government has "no idea whatever" of devaluing the pound sterling. Devaluation would "increase the price of our imports and decrease the price of exports, which is exactly the opposite of what we are trying to accomplish."

Oct. 5, 1948—"Devaluation is neither advisable nor even possible in present conditions."

Dec. 31, 1948—"No one need fear devaluation of our currency in any circumstances."

April 30, 1949—"Sterling revaluation is neither necessary nor will it take place."

June 28, 1949—"There has been no pressure on me by America to devalue the pound."

July 6, 1949—"The government has not the slightest intention of devaluing the pound."

July 14, 1949—"No suggestion was made at the conference [with Snyder and Abbott] . . . that sterling be devalued. And that, I hope, is that."

Sept. 6, 1949—"I will stick to the . . . statement I made [July 14] in the House of Commons."

In brief, Sir Stafford emphatically denied at least a dozen times that he would do what he did. The excuse has been made for him that naturally he could not afford to admit any such intention in advance because no one would then have accepted sterling at $4.03. This "defense" amounts to saying that unless the government had lied it could not have successfully deceived the buyers of British goods and the holders of sterling.

For this is what "devaluation" means. It is a confession of bankruptcy. To announce that IOU's hitherto guaranteed to be worth $4.03 are in fact worth only $2.80 is to tell your creditors that their old claims on you are now worth no more than 70 cents on the dollar.

When a private individual announces bankruptcy, he is thought to be disgraced. When a government does so, it acts as if it had brought off a brilliant coup. This is what our own government did in 1933 when it jauntily repudiated its promises to redeem its currency in gold. Here is how the *London Bankers' Magazine* described the 1949 devaluation of the pound by the British Government: "The political technique for dealing with these issues has worn thin. It consists of strenuous, even vicious repudiation beforehand of any notion of revaluation. It insists that the move would be ineffective and utters portentous warning about the dangers. When the unthinkable happens the public is slapped on the back and congratulated on the best piece of luck it has encountered for years."

This is what governments have now been doing for a generation. This is what "monetary management" really means. In practice it is merely a high-sounding euphemism for continuous currency debasement. It consists of constant lying in order to support constant swindling. Instead of automatic currencies based on gold, people are forced to take managed currencies based on guile. Instead of precious metals they hold paper promises whose value falls with every bureaucratic whim. And they are suavely assured that only hopelessly antiquated minds dream of returning to truth and honesty and solvency and gold.

24

9

Gold Goes With Freedom

The question whether or not it is desirable to return to a real gold standard, and when, and under what conditions, and at what rate, and by precisely what steps, has become extremely complicated. But an excellent contribution to the subject was made in a speech of W. Randolph Burgess, then chairman of the executive committee of the National City Bank of New York, before the American Bankers Association in November of 1949. I quote in part:

"Historically one of the best protections of the value of money against the inroads of political spending was the gold standard—the redemption of money in gold on demand. This put a check-rein on the politician. For inflationary spending led to the loss of gold either by exports or by withdrawals by individuals who distrusted government policies. This was a kind of automatic limit on credit expansion. . . .

"Of course the modern economic planners don't like the gold standard just because it does put a limit on their powers. . . . I have great confidence that the world will return to the gold standard in some form because the people in so many countries have learned that they need protection from the excesses of their political leaders. . . .

"There is a group of people today asking for the restoration of the full gold standard immediately in the United States. Today we have a dollar that is convertible into gold for foreign governments and central banks; these people are asking for the same rights to hold gold for our own citizens. In principle I believe these people are right, though I think they are wrong in their timing, and overemphasize the immediate benefits. . . .

"If you try to force the pace by resuming gold payments before the foundations are laid through government policies on the budget, on credit, and on prices, the gold released may simply move out into hoards and become the tool of the speculator.

"Gold payments are only part of the building of sound money, and they are in a sense the capstone of the arch. . . ."

The great virtue of this statement is not only that it recognizes the central importance of returning to a real gold standard but that it takes account also of the formidable difficulties that our past and present errors and sins have placed in the way.

The gold standard is not important as an isolated gadget but only as an integral part of a whole economic system. Just as "managed" paper money goes with a statist and collectivist philosophy, with government "planning," with a coercive economy in which the citizen is always at the mercy of bureaucratic caprice, so the gold standard is an integral part of a free-enterprise economy under which governments respect private property, economize in spending, balance their budgets, keep their promises, and refuse to connive in overexpansion of money or credit. Until our government is prepared to return to this system in its entirety and has given evidence of this intention by its deeds, it is pointless to try to force it to go on a real gold basis. For it would only be off again in a few months. And, as in the past, the gold standard itself, rather than the abuses that destroyed it, would get the popular blame.

In the preceding chapter I recited the shabby record of Sir Stafford Cripps, not as a personal criticism but as an illustration of what typically, if not inevitably, happens under a "managed" paper-money system. For Sir Stafford was not the lowest type of politician likely to be entrusted to manage the people's money; he was the highest type. To millions he had been the very symbol of political integrity and courage. "If gold ruste," as Chaucer asked, "what shal iren do?"

Which reminds us that real gold doesn't rust. As a currency basis it may lack one or two of the perfections that theorists dream of, but it weighs more and can be kept longer than a politician's pledge.

10

In Dispraise of Paper

A speech by Allan Sproul, then president of the Federal Reserve Bank of New York, before the American Bankers Association in 1949, was a startling revelation of official doctrine.

"I perceive," said Sproul, "no moral problem involved in this question of gold convertibility." Let's see whether we cannot perhaps perceive one. Prior to the year 1933 our government pledged itself to pay interest and principal on its bonds in gold of a specified weight and fineness. It also pledged the holder of every currency note that it would redeem that note on demand in gold of a specified weight and fineness. It violated its most solemn pledge. It deprived the rightful owners of their gold. And it made the possession of gold by anybody but the thief illegal.

Now our monetary managers tell us how lucky we are at last to have a system at home of irredeemable paper. Sproul sings paeans in praise of paper. "We use a paper money," he says, "which has the supreme attribute of general acceptability." He neglects to add—at a constantly falling value. The purchasing power of a paper dollar in 1949, according to the Department of Commerce, was only 52 cents, as measured by wholesale prices, in terms of the 1935-39 dollar. It is now only 43 cents by the same measure.

Sproul resorts to flag waving. "The integrity of our money does not depend on domestic gold convertibility. It depends upon the great productive power of the American economy. . . ." Those who recall the disastrous paper money inflations of history must shiver at this argument. Listen to Andrew D. White's report of speeches made in the French Assembly in 1791 to defend the paper assignats: " 'Fear nothing; your currency reposes upon a sound mortgage.' Then followed a glorification of the patriotism of the French people, which, he asserted, would carry the nation through all its difficulties."

The nub of Sproul's defense of our internal irredeemability is that the bureaucrats must be trusted implicitly but that the people cannot be trusted at all. It appears that when you allow the people to redeem their money in gold they always want to do it at the wrong time—i.e., just when it is most embarrassing for the government to meet the demand; in other words, just when the government has connived in an inflationary expansion and issued more paper claims than it is able to honor.

"The principal argument for restoring the circulation of gold coin," Sproul declares, "seems to be distrust of the money managers and of the fiscal policies of government." He couldn't have said it better. What he fails to see is that this mistrust has been richly earned. In addition to the shabby record of Sir Stafford Cripps, we need to remind ourselves that some 30 governments instantly followed the

British example. They wiped out overnight, by simple ukase, part of the value of every paper currency unit in the hands of their own people.

Yet in the face of this almost universal record of currency debasement (not to bring up our own sorry record of currency inflation since 1933), Sproul can seriously speak of leaving everything to what he calls "competent and responsible men." Said Sir Stafford Cripps, in explaining his devaluation record: "Even if we had then had some future intention of altering the rate of exchange, which in fact we had not, no responsible minister could possibly have done otherwise than deny such intention." Here, then, is an authoritative definition. A "competent and responsible" monetary manager is one who not only lies to his people regarding the future of their currency but even considers it his *duty* to deceive them.

Sproul's currency theory may be summed up thus: Put your faith in the monetary managers, who have always fooled you in the past.

11

Inflation and High "Costs"

In an earlier chapter I declared that inflation, always and everywhere, is primarily caused by an increase in the supply of money and credit.

There is nothing peculiar or particularly original about this statement. It corresponds closely, in fact, with "orthodox" doctrine. It is supported overwhelmingly by theory, experience, and statistics.

But this simple explanation meets with considerable resistance. Politicians deny or ignore it, because it places responsibility for inflation squarely on their own policies. Few of the academic economists are helpful. Most of them attribute present inflation to a complicated and disparate assortment of factors and "pressures." Labor leaders vaguely attribute inflation to the "greed" or "exorbitant profits" of manufacturers. And most businessmen have been similarly eager to pass the buck. The retailer throws the blame for higher prices on the exactions of the wholesaler, the wholesaler on the manufacturer, and the manufacturer on the raw-material supplier and on labor costs.

This last view is still widespread. Few manufacturers are students of money and banking; the total supply of currency and bank deposits is something that seems highly abstract to most of them and remote from their immediate experience. As one of them once wrote to me: "The thing that increases prices is costs."

What he did not seem to realize is that a "cost" is simply another name for a price. One of the consequences of the division of labor is that everybody's price is somebody else's cost, and vice versa. The price of pig iron is the steelmaker's cost. The steelmaker's price is the automobile manufacturer's cost. The automobile manufacturer's price is the doctor's or the taxicab-operating company's cost. And so on. Nearly all costs, it is true, ultimately resolve themselves into salaries or wages. But weekly salaries or hourly wages are the "price" that most of us get for our services.

Now inflation, which is an increase in the supply of money, lowers the value of the monetary unit. This is another way of saying that it raises both prices and "costs." And "costs" do not necessarily go up sooner than prices do. Ham may go up before hogs, and hogs before corn. It is a mistake to conclude, with the old Ricardian economists, that prices are determined by costs of production. It would be just as true to say that costs of production are determined by prices. What hog raisers can afford to bid for corn, for example, depends on the price they are getting for hogs.

In the short run, both prices and costs are determined by the relationships of supply and demand—including, of course, the supply of money as well as goods. It is true that in the long run there is a constant tendency for prices to equal marginal costs of production. This is because, though what a thing *has* cost cannot determine its price, what it *now* costs or is *expected* to cost will determine how much of it, if any, will be made.

If these relationships were better understood, fewer editorial writers would attribute inflation to the so-called "wage-price spiral." In itself, a wage boost (above the "equilibrium" level) does not lead to inflation but to unemployment. The wage boost can, of course (and under present political pressures usually does), lead to more inflation *indirectly* by leading to an increase in the money supply to make the wage boost payable. But it is the increase in the money supply that causes the inflation. Not until we clearly recognize this will we know how to bring inflation to a halt.

12

Is Inflation a Blessing?

The late Sumner H. Slichter, professor of economics at
Harvard, was a clear, vigorous, able, and highly influential
writer. He made many instructive contributions, but in the
field of money and inflation, to which he mainly devoted
himself in the last years of his life, I cannot believe that his
influence was for the good. I take as one example an article
by him in *Harper's Magazine* of August, 1952, under the
title "How Bad Is Inflation?" This article, in fact, seemed
to epitomize all the shopworn fallacies that have been put
forward as apologies for inflation in the last two centuries.

Professor Slichter began by dismissing the conclusions on
inflation by the American Assembly, a group of distin-
guished economists, as "uncritical and almost hysterical."
The assembly concluded that "inflation is a continuous and
serious threat to the stability of the American economy and
to the security of the entire Western world." This judgment
was not hysterical, but restrained.

It was Slichter who was appallingly uncritical. He not
only thought that it is easy for a government to plan and
control "a slow rise in prices"; he actually believed that an
"extreme" inflation "is not easily started." It would be inter-

esting to learn what his definition was of an "extreme" inflation, and what his concept was of difficulty. Germany inflated until its mark fell to one-trillionth of its previous value. Nationalist China inflated until the yuan reached 425 million to the dollar. In Great Britain prices at the time this *Harper's* article appeared were three times as high as they were before World War II; in the Argentine (with no "war" excuse) prices were already five to eight times as high; in France, more than 25 times as high; in Italy, more than 50 times as high. None of these countries found it at all difficult to get its inflation going, but most of them were finding it politically almost impossible to stop.

Slichter's argument throughout was based on assumptions that are neither proved nor warranted. One of these is that a rising price level is necessary for prosperity. This is refuted by a wealth of historical experience. The great American boom from 1925 to 1929, for example, occurred in spite of a *falling* price level. And Slichter did not seem to remember that depressions are caused chiefly by the collapse of previous inflations.

Nor did Slichter seem to understand how inflation temporarily works its magic. It does so only as long as prices run ahead of costs (mainly wages). Then the prospective restoration or increase of profit margins may lead to an increase in production and employment. But the jig is up once labor gets on to the game, and wages and other costs begin to rise faster than prices. The apostles of permanent inflation ("continuous slow" inflation) are those who believe that labor can be permanently fooled.

Slichter did not explain in his article by exactly what

35

process a "slow" permanent rise in prices—say 2 or 3 per cent a year—could be produced. He did not understand why no nation has yet succeeded in keeping an inflation, once started, under control. He forgot that you can't afford to tell people in advance that you are *planning* to cheat them. A government can't *plan* a "gradual" increase in prices, because if people *know* that prices will be 3 per cent higher, say, next year, they will bid prices up nearly that much right away. If creditors *know* that the purchasing power of the money they are asked to lend today is going to depreciate 3 per cent within a year, they will add 3 per cent to whatever interest rate they would otherwise demand; so that instead of lending at 5 per cent, say, they will ask 8.

Most astonishing of all, Slichter advocated a continuous inflation to *combat* Communism. One might have referred him to the late Lord Keynes, who wrote a generation ago: "Lenin is said to have declared that the best way to destroy the capitalist system was to debauch the currency. Lenin was certainly right. The process engages all the hidden forces of economic law on the side of destruction, and does it in a manner which not one man in a million is able to diagnose."

Slichter, alas, was not that one man.

Why Return to Gold?

Fifty years ago practically every economist of repute supported the gold standard. Most of the merits of that standard were clearly recognized. It was, for one thing, international. When the currency unit of nearly every major country was defined as a specified weight of gold (previous to 1934 the American dollar, for example, was defined as 23.22 grains of fine gold), every such currency unit bore a fixed relation to every other currency unit of the same kind. It was convertible at that fixed ratio, on demand, to any amount, and by anybody who held it, into any other gold currency unit. The result was in effect an international currency system. Gold was the international medium of exchange.

This international gold standard was the chief safeguard against tampering with the currency on the part of politicians and bureaucrats. It was the chief safeguard against domestic inflation. When credit inflation did occur, it produced a quick sequence of results. Domestic prices rose. This encouraged imports and discouraged exports. The balance of trade (or payments) shifted "against" the inflating country. Gold started to flow out. This caused a contraction of the bank credit based on the gold, and brought the inflation to a halt.

Usually, in fact, the chain of consequences was shorter, quicker, and more direct. As soon as foreign bankers and exchange dealers even suspected the existence of inflation in a given country, the exchange rate for that country's currency fell "below the gold point." Gold started to flow out. Then the central-bank managers of the country that was losing gold raised the discount rate. The effect was not merely to halt credit expansion at home, but to draw funds from abroad from lenders who wanted to take advantage of the higher short-term interest rates. The gold flow was stopped or reversed.

Thus so long as the gold standard was resolutely maintained, a whole set of related benefits ensued. Domestic currency tampering and anything more than a relatively moderate inflation were impossible. As gold convertibility had to be maintained at all times, confidence had to be maintained not only through every year but every day. Unsound monetary and economic policies, or even serious proposals of unsound policies, were immediately reflected in exchange rates and in gold movements. The unsound policies or proposals, therefore, had to be quickly moderated or abandoned.

Because there was a fixed and dependable exchange ratio as well as free convertibility between one currency unit and another, international trade, lending, and investment were undertaken freely and with confidence. And, finally, the international gold standard established (apart from differences caused by shipping costs and tariffs) uniform world prices for transportable commodities—wheat, coffee, sugar, cotton, wool, lead, copper, silver, etc.

It has become fashionable to say that in a major crisis, such as war, the gold standard "breaks down." But except to the extent that the citizens of a country fear invasion, conquest, and physical seizure of their gold by the enemy, this is an untrue description of what happens. It is not that the gold standard "breaks down," but that it is deliberately abandoned or destroyed. What the citizens of a country really fear in such crises is inflation by their own monetary managers, or seizure of their gold by their own bureaucrats. This inflation or seizure is not "inevitable" in wartime; it is the result of policy.

In short, it is precisely the merits of the international gold standard which the world's money managers and bureaucrats decry. They do not want to be prevented from inflating whenever they see fit to inflate. They do not want their domestic economy and prices to be tied into the world economy and world prices. They want to be free to manipulate their own domestic price level. They want to pursue purely nationalistic policies (at the expense or imagined expense of other countries), and their pretenses to "internationalism" are a pious fraud.

14

Gold Means Good Faith

Nothing has more clearly demonstrated the need for the gold standard than its abandonment. Since that occurred, in Britain in 1931 and in the United States in 1933, the world has been plunged, both in wartime and in peacetime, into a sea of paper money and unending inflation.

Although the inflation everywhere has been blamed on "the war," it has occurred in nations that were never involved in the war (throughout Latin America, for example), and it has continued to rage since the war ended. As an indirect index of this, wholesale prices have increased in this country 86 per cent since 1945; in Britain more than 100 per cent; in France 810 per cent.* And everywhere this result has been due primarily to the increase in the paper money supply.

The monetary managers are fond of telling us that they have substituted "responsible monetary management" for the gold standard. But there is no historic record of responsible paper-money management. Here and there it is possible to point to brief periods of "stabilization" of paper money. But such periods have always been precarious and

* Before the introduction of the "heavy franc," at the beginning of 1960, at a valuation of 100 old francs.

short-lived. The record taken as a whole is one of hyper-inflation, devaluation, and monetary chaos. And as for any integrity in paper-money management, we need merely recall the record of Sir Stafford Cripps, who, in the two-year period preceding his devaluation of the pound sterling on September 18, 1949, publicly denied any such possibility no fewer than a dozen times.

This is what happens under monetary management without the discipline of the gold standard. The gold standard not only helps to ensure good policy and good faith; its own continuance or resumption requires good policy and good faith. If I may repeat what I pointed out in Chapter 9: The gold standard is not important as an isolated gadget but only as an integral part of the whole economic system. Just as "managed" paper money goes with a statist and collectivist philosophy, with government "planning," with a coercive economy in which the citizen is always at the mercy of bureaucratic caprice, so the gold standard is an integral part of a free-enterprise economy under which governments respect private property, economize in spending, balance their budgets, keep their promises, and above all refuse to connive in inflation—in the overexpansion of money or credit.

So if, as it should, the American government decides to return to a full gold standard, its first step must be to bring inflation to a halt. Without this preliminary or accompanying step any attempted return to gold would be certain to collapse. And once again the gold standard itself, rather than the inflation, would probably be discredited in the popular mind.

How, then, does one halt inflation? The economist Ludwig von Mises has maintained that no increase whatever should be allowed in the quantity of money and bank credit that is not 100 per cent covered by deposits paid in by the public. Although this is basically the result that should be aimed at, it would be politically more acceptable, I think, if this result were brought about by means in accordance with our own best practices and past traditions. I therefore suggest that the halting of inflation should be achieved by these four means:

1—Start balancing the budget.

2—Stop using the banking system either to buy and peg government bonds at fixed rates, or as a dumping ground for huge new issues of short-term government securities. (The peacetime rule, in fact, might be to permit no further net increase in the total volume of government securities held by the country's banking system.)

3—Insist that the Federal Reserve Banks impose discount rates that would penalize borrowing by member banks rather than make it profitable. This means that the rediscount rate should be kept above the rate to prime borrowing customers at the great city banks.

4—Restore the legal reserve requirements of the Federal Reserve Banks (over a reasonable time period) to 40 per cent from their "war emergency" reserve level of only 25 per cent adopted in 1945 (or from whatever still lower gold reserve requirement exists at the time of the reform). There is no more effective way in which Congress could register its own opposition to further inflation.

15

What Price for Gold?

Granted that it is desirable, and even imperative, to return to a full gold standard, by what methods should we return? And at precisely what dollar-gold ratio—i.e., at what "price for gold"? These difficult problems have split into dissident groups even the minority of economists who are actively urging a return to a gold standard.

One group, for example, contends that we can and should return to a full gold standard immediately, and at the present price of $35 an ounce. It bases this contention on the arguments that we are already on a limited gold standard at that rate (foreign central banks, at least, are permitted to buy gold from us and sell it to us at $35 an ounce); that we should not suspend this limited gold standard even as a transitional step for a few months; that in the interests of good faith and stability there should be "no further tampering" with this rate; and that at this rate we would in fact have a large enough gold reserve to maintain full convertibility against present outstanding paper currency and deposit liabilities.

These arguments, however, rest on debatable assumptions. Some superficial comparisons, it is true, seem to support

43

them. At the beginning of 1933, the United States money supply (time and demand bank deposits plus currency outside of banks) was $44.9 billion, and the country's gold holdings (measured at the old rate of $20.67 an ounce) were $4.2 billion, or only 9.4 per cent of the country's money supply. At the end of 1963 our outstanding money supply was $265 billion, and our gold holdings against it (measured at the current rate of $35 an ounce) were $15.6 billion, or less than 6 per cent.

Thus our gold reserve ratio is less than in 1933. And we were *thrown off* gold in 1933.

In writing this, I recognize that the run on gold, at the particular moment at which it took place, was at least in part precipitated by the growth of uncontradicted rumors and press reports that the Roosevelt Administration was planning to suspend gold payments. Nevertheless, the relation of credit volume and commodity prices to gold at that time was still such that we had only the choice of going off gold, which we did; or devaluing the dollar and staying on gold (i.e., raising the official gold price); or suffering still further stagnation and deflation. In any case, the run on gold in 1933, before payments were suspended, means that the gold reserves at that time were not in fact sufficient, *in relation to other conditions,* to maintain confidence.

Present gold reserve comparisons with past periods must take account, moreover, of changes in the relative percentage of the world's gold supply held in the United States. In

44

December 1926, the United States held 45 per cent of the world's monetary gold supply (excluding Russia); in December 1933 it held only 33.6 per cent. In 1953 it held 60.8 per cent. At the end of 1959 it held 48.3 per cent. If the United States *alone* returned to gold it could conceivably continue to hold an abnormal percentage for a certain time. But if other countries followed suit within a few years (which would be both desirable and probable), they would presumably attract their previous proportion of the world's gold. More immediately important: In mid-1964, against our gold holdings of $15.5 billion, short-term liabilities to foreigners reported by American banks came to $26.3 billion. And the United States was still showing a heavy deficit in its international balance of payments.

But the real error of those who think we could safely return to a full gold standard at a rate of only $35 an ounce lies in the assumption that there is some fixed "normal" percentage of gold reserves to outstanding money liabilities that is entirely safe under all conditions. This, in fact, is not true of any gold reserve of less than 100 per cent. In periods when public confidence exists in the determination of the monetary managers to maintain the gold standard, as well as in the prudence and wisdom of their policy, gold convertibility may be maintained with a surprisingly low reserve. But when confidence in the wisdom, prudence, and good faith of the monetary managers has been shaken, a

45

gold reserve far above "normal" will be required to maintain convertibility. And today confidence in the wisdom, prudence, and good faith of the world's monetary managers has been all but destroyed. It may take years of wisdom, prudence, and good faith to restore it. Until that is done, any effort to resume a full gold standard at $35 an ounce might lead to a panicky run on gold, while a determined effort to maintain that rate might precipitate a violent deflation.

16

The Dollar-Gold Ratio

The gold-standard supporters are divided into three main groups: (1) those who think we could safely return to a full gold standard at $35 an ounce; (2) those who urge return to a full gold standard at some specific higher price for gold (e.g., $70 an ounce) which they claim they already know to be the "correct" one; and (3) those who recommend that we permit a temporary free market in gold for guidance in fixing a final dollar-gold conversion rate.

I have already discussed the main arguments of those who urge a return to gold at $35 an ounce, and what I consider to be some of the shortcomings of those arguments. Those who are urging that we set the price of gold at a higher figure, and who claim to know already what that figure should be, commonly base their conclusion on some comparison of price levels. For example, since 1932, the last full year in which we were on a real gold basis (at $20.67 an ounce), wholesale prices have increased 203 per cent. On the argument that only a corresponding increase in the price of gold could prevent a fall in prices if we went back to a full gold standard, the new price of gold would have to be about $63. Again, the price of gold was set at $35 an ounce on

47

January 31, 1934. For the next seven years wholesale prices averaged only 40 per cent of their present level. If we assume that $35 was the "right" price of gold in those seven years—1934-40—then the price of gold necessary to maintain the present wholesale price level might have to be about $87.

The dubious nature of the assumptions behind such calculations is clear. But the rate at which we return to a full gold standard is not a matter of indifference. Charles Rist, one of the world's leading monetary economists, argued in a powerful article in *Foreign Affairs* in April 1934 that one of the major causes of the world crisis of 1929-33 was the attempt of leading countries, including the United States, to maintain or return to gold convertibility at their prewar rate for gold after having enormously multiplied their paper currency circulation.

The case of Great Britain is clear. It had gone off gold in World War I. The pound had dropped from a gold parity of $4.86 to a low of $3.18 in February 1920, and had returned in late 1924 to approximately 10 per cent below the gold parity. But wholesale prices in Britain in 1924 were still 70 per cent above their prewar level. The British Government decided to resume the gold standard at the old par in 1925. The result was a steady fall in wholesale prices over the next seven years from an index number of 171.1 (1913 equals 100) in January 1925 to 99.2 in September 1931, the month in which England abandoned the gold standard. As the British all during this period were unwilling to make corresponding cuts in retail prices and wage rates, the result was falling exports, stagnation, and unemployment. And it

48

was the gold standard itself, not the false rate (or the internal inflexibility of wages), that got the blame.

The British repeated this pattern in essence in the summer of 1947, when they tried to make the pound convertible into the dollar at the wholly unrealistic rate of $4.03. When that experiment broke down within a few weeks, the British once more blamed convertibility itself, and not the false rate, for the breakdown.

It is of the highest importance not only to our own economic future, but to the future of the world, that we do not repeat the British errors by trying to return to gold convertibility at an overvaluation of the paper dollar (which would mean an undervaluation of gold). A temporary free market in gold would give us more guidance regarding what the new conversion rate should be than either an adamant insistence on $35 an ounce or some dubious calculation based largely on hypothetical assumptions.

17

Lesson of the Greenbacks

One of the worst consequences of inflation is that most of its mischiefs and injustices are irreparable. They cannot be cured by deflation. This merely brings about its own hardships and injustices, which are just as likely to fall upon the previous victims of inflation as upon its beneficiaries. We cannot, for example, cure the inflationary erosion or wiping out of the purchasing power of savings-bank deposits, government bonds and insurance policies by a deflation which may bring about the unemployment or bankruptcy of the very people who suffered from the inflation. So when an inflation has gone beyond a certain amount, the best we can do is to try to stabilize at the new level. When an inflation has gone to the lengths of that in Germany in 1923, for example, or that in France today, a return to the pre-inflation level is inconceivable.

Just what should be attempted, therefore, after an inflation has passed a certain point, becomes an awkward practical problem to which there simply cannot be any completely "just" or satisfactory solution.

We have seen in the preceding chapter what happened in Britain when it tried to go back to the gold standard at the old parity in 1925. But there are many who believe that our own resumption of gold payments on January 1, 1879, at the prewar parity, after the paper money inflation of the Civil War, was an unalloyed success. The fears of a gold drain, they argue, proved quite unfounded. And they attribute the subsequent American recovery of 1879 largely or wholly to gold resumption.

A closer examination of the whole inflationary and deflationary period from 1862 to 1879, however, tells a different story. As soon as the government started issuing irredeemable "greenbacks" in 1862, gold went to a premium on the open market and commodity prices started to soar. In 1864, the greenbacks fell as low as 35 cents on the dollar in terms of gold. From 1860 to 1865, inclusive, though the average of European prices rose only 4 to 6 per cent, average prices in the United States advanced no less than 116 per cent.

But immediately after the end of the war, American prices started downward. At first this was politically popular, because wages had not yet advanced as much as the cost of living. But after 1866 wages had more than caught up with prices. The continued fall in prices soon began to cause bankruptcies and unemployment. Finally came the panic of 1873 which, in the measured judgment of some economists, "left the country's financial and commercial structure almost a ruin." The causes of the panic were complex. But one of them was certainly the continued fall of commodity prices that accompanied the rise of the greenbacks toward parity. By 1873 the greenbacks were only about 15 per cent below parity, and wholesale prices were down to about 30 per cent above prewar levels.

The result of the panic of 1873 was greatly to increase inflationist sentiment. It is true that the Resumption Act was passed on January 7, 1875, but by a repudiated lame-duck Republican Congress that had nothing more to lose. Even more ironic, it was passed, the economist J. Laurence Laughlin tells us, "only under the delusion that it was an inflation measure," because "on its face it looked like a bill to expand the national bank circulation."

Many commentators today think it was foolish and need-less for the Resumption Act to put off the actual day of resumption to January 1, 1879—four years after passage of the act. They forget, however, that time, skill, and determination were required to accumulate a gold reserve which would inspire so much confidence that gold would not be demanded when the day of redemption came. And they forget, too, that returning to gold at the original parity involved a still further decline (of about 30 per cent) in American commodity prices to bring them into line with world gold prices. This decline actually took place between 1875 and 1879, and the whole period was one of "economy and liquidation." In 1878, for example, the record of insolvencies far exceeded even that of the panic year 1873.

Many commentators today attribute the recovery that came in the second half of 1879 to the return to gold redemption. The facts do not support them. "With hardly an exception," writes the economic historian, Alexander D. Noyes, "the country's staple industries sank, during the early months of 1879, into complete stagnation." What suddenly turned the tide was an unparalleled coincidence: Europe suffered the worst crop disaster in many years, whereas the

American wheat crop reached a new high record. This meant high prices and crop exports unparalleled up to that time.

All this is not to argue that after the greenback inflation of the Civil War this country should have returned to gold at a lower parity for the dollar. It is simply to point out that we had to pay a heavy price for the course we actually took, even though our economy was far more flexible then than now, particularly as regards wage-rates. We must take care that when we return to gold this time we do so at a rate that involves neither inflation nor serious deflation.

18

The Black Market Test

It may perhaps be argued that the collapse of the attempted return by Britain in 1925 to the old gold parity, or the hardships involved in the American resumption of specie payments after the Civil War, are irrelevant to the present problem of the United States because (1) we are already on a de facto gold standard at $35 an ounce so far as foreign central banks are concerned, and (2) even in the black market the price of gold bullion has sometimes been no higher than $35 an ounce.

These arguments have some weight, but they are far from conclusive.

As regards the first argument, it may be pointed out that our restricted gold standard at $35 an ounce has been maintained only in a highly abnormal world situation that cannot be counted on to continue. It would, in fact, prove ultimately disastrous if it continued. For even this token American gold standard has been tenable only because the United States has for twenty-six years been the *least unsafe* place for gold, and because most other leading countries have inflated even more. A slight shift in this situation could easily lead to a heavy drain on American gold. There has been a substantial drain on our gold, in fact, since the high point of $24.5 billion was reached in 1949.

The better the monetary behavior of foreign countries becomes, in other words, the more precarious will become the maintenance even of our closely restricted gold standard at $35 an ounce. And this $35 an ounce standard might give way entirely if private citizens, private businessmen and private bankers, American and foreign, were as free to demand gold for their notes as are foreign central banks. In fact, it is this very fear that is used to justify the present prohibitions against gold convertibility for the private citizen.

As regards the second argument, I do not believe that the black market price of gold bullion, under present circumstances (gold *coins* are still at a premium), is a reliable guide to anything in particular. There are innumerable possible leaks between the American buying-and-selling rate of $35 an ounce, and the black market, which make the former dominate and control the latter. (The American Federal Reserve Banks feed out gold to the Bank of England to help it hold down the "free" London market price.)

There are more than a hundred member nations in the International Monetary Fund. How can the American Federal Reserve System, or the I.M.F., supervise and police them all?—not to speak of individual officials in them? Many of these member nations are very poor; it would help their position, or the position of their central banks, if they could buy gold at $35 an ounce from the American Federal Reserve and resell it to private individuals in their own country at a premium. If something like this were going on, even in a few instances, it would mean the existence of "arbitrage" transactions which would prevent more than a moderate spread between the black market and the official market.

I am not framing this as an accusation, but simply as an illustration of one way in which the disappearance of the former black market premium on gold bars could be accounted for. Nicolaas C. Havenga, the South African Minister of Finance, and the eminent French economist, the late Charles Rist, have both implied, in fact, that a sufficient explanation of the disappearance of the black market premium price is that the demand for gold is still subjected almost everywhere to legal restrictions and prohibitions, while the available supply has been becoming more and more abundant. In any case, it would be a very dubious inference to take the absence of a black market premium as any guarantee of the "rightness" or tenability of the present official $35 price.

And certainly any such coincidence of price is not a valid argument for continuing to prohibit a truly free American and world market in gold. The reason free markets in gold do not exist under a full gold standard is not because they are forbidden, but because the universal ability of everyone to buy or sell gold at the official rate leaves no need for a free market. Under a full gold standard, a free market would have nothing to do, no purpose to serve, no function to perform. It is needed only under a paper-money standard, or under a discriminatory and half-fictitious "gold standard" of the sort the United States has had since 1934. It is precisely when a free gold market is needed that most modern governments seek to suppress it. For it reflects and measures the extent of the lack of confidence in the domestic currency; and it exposes the fictitious quality of the "official" rate. And these are among the very reasons why it is needed.

19

How to Return to Gold

If we grant that there is a great potential danger in trying to return immediately to a full gold standard at $35 an ounce, by what steps are we to return? And how are we to determine the dollar-gold ratio—which would decide the new "price of gold"—at which the return should be made?

It is a sound general principle that unless there are the strongest reasons for change, the dollar-gold ratio, once fixed, ought not to be tampered with. This rule certainly applied to the pre-1933 rate of $20.67 an ounce, because that was a real rate, at which anybody was entitled to demand gold, and got it. But the $35 rate, fixed by Roosevelt-Morgenthau whim in 1934, is not a rate at which real convertibility has existed. It is only foreign central banks, not American citizens, that have been permitted to buy gold from our Federal Reserve Banks at $35 an ounce, and even they have been allowed to do this only under certain conditions. The present $35-an-ounce gold standard is a window-dressing standard, a mere gold-*plated* standard. There is no reason for treating the $35 figure as sacrosanct.

The new dollar-gold ratio that we should aim at is one at which gold convertibility can be permanently maintained, and that will not be in itself either inflationary or deflationary—that will neither, in other words, in itself bring about a rise or a fall in prices.

There are some economists who contend on unconvincing evidence that $35 an ounce *is* that rate. Others profess to have some mathematical formula for arriving at such a rate, and on this basis confidently advocate $70 an ounce or some other figure. Their diverse results in themselves invite suspicion. Values and prices are not set by mathematical calculations, but by supply and demand operating through free markets.

Because of the enormous inflation in the thirty years since we departed from a real gold standard, and the enormous shock to confidence that inflations, devaluations, and repudiations have produced, we must test the state of confidence in a temporary free market for gold—a market that will also give us a guide to a new dollar-gold ratio that we can hold.

The following time schedule of gold resumption is put forward chiefly for purposes of illustration:

1—The Administration will immediately announce its intention to return to a full gold standard by a series of steps dated in advance. The Federal Reserve Banks and the Treasury will temporarily suspend all sales or purchases of gold, merely holding on to what they have. Simultaneously with this step, a free market in gold will be permitted.

2—After watching this market, and meanwhile preventing any further inflation, the government, within a period of not more than a year, will announce the dollar-gold ratio at which convertibility will take place.

3—On and after Convertibility Day, and for the following six months, any holder of dollars will be entitled to convert them into gold bars, but at a moderate discount on the paper dollars he turns in. To put the matter the other way, he would be asked to pay a premium on gold bars above the new valuation—equivalent, let us say, to ½ of 1 per cent a month. The purpose of this would be to spread out the first demands for conversion and discourage excessive pressure on reserves at the beginning. The same purpose could be achieved also by a wide but gradually narrowing spread between the official buying and selling prices of gold bars. Of course, the free market in gold would continue during this period, and if gold could be obtained in this free market for less than the official premium rates, it would not be demanded from the government's reserves.

4—Six months after Convertibility Day, the country will return to a full gold-bullion standard. Conversion of dollars into gold bars, or vice versa, will be open to all holders without such discounts or premiums and without discrimination.

5—One year later still, on January 1, 19—, the country will return to a full gold-coin standard, by minting gold coins and permitting free conversion.

A full gold-coin standard is desirable because a gold-bullion standard is merely a rich man's standard. A relatively poor man should be just as able to protect himself against inflation, to the extent of his dollar holdings, as a rich man. The reason for returning to a full gold-coin standard in several stages is to prevent too sudden a drain on gold reserves before confidence has been re-established.

We achieved this end after the Civil War by delaying actual resumption for four years after passage of the Resumption Act. A program like the foregoing would provide a faster schedule.

20

Some Errors of Inflationists

In every year of the past quarter-century of inflation articulate individuals or groups have insisted that we were in fact in a depression or a deflation, or on the verge of one, or at the very least that our "economic growth" was not as fast as the adoption of their particular inflationist schemes could make it.

A typical example is a "report" of the National Planning Association (a group of statist planners who frequently manage to get their pronouncements on the front pages of leading newspapers) in mid-1954. This report declared that the country must step up its production of goods and services by "at least $25 billion" over the next twelve months to keep the economy healthy. Why, as long as they were simply talking about what was desirable, they stopped at a mere $25 billion, I do not know.

The pronouncement, however, was so typical of current inflationist fallacies that it is worth a little analysis. The NPA firmly believed that what primarily caused the "recession" from mid-1953 to mid-1954 was a drop in defense spending, and therefore what could pull us out was a boost in defense spending. Such a judgment, however, finds no support in either economic theory or experience. In the fiscal year 1944 the Federal government spent $95 billion; in the fiscal year 1947 it spent $39 billion. Here was a drop in the annual Federal spending rate in this three-year period of $56 billion. Yet, far from there being a recession in this three-year period, there was a substantial increase in employment, wages, and prices.

I may add that there was a very sharp increase in industrial production and employment between mid-1954 and mid-1955—though in that fiscal year total Federal spending, instead of being increased (as recommended by NPA), was further reduced by more than $3 billion.

This fact did not escape the notice of observers at the time. In a column in *The New York Times* of September 8, 1955, Arthur Krock drew attention to official statistics which showed that private spending in the United States had been steadily replacing, and in fact exceeding, the billions cut from the budget by the Eisenhower Administration over a two-year period. The following table shows the comparison:

	1953	1954	1955
Gross national product	$369.3	$357.6	$384.8
Federal purchases of goods and services	61.0	48.6	45.2
All other expenditures	308.3	309.0	339.6

What is really compared in the foregoing table is the second quarters of 1953, 1954, and 1955. The figures are expressed, however, in billions of dollars at seasonally adjusted annual rates. They show that while government spending was running at an annual rate of $3.4 billion less in the 1955 quarter than in 1954, and $15.8 billion less than

63

in the corresponding 1953 quarter, nongovernmental activity was running in the second quarter of 1955 at a rate $30.6 billion higher than in the same period of 1954 and $31.3 billion higher than in 1953.

There is really nothing astonishing in such figures except to those who tenaciously hold to a quite erroneous preconceived view. Yet again and again in recent years we find it stated or assumed by business "forecasters" that the future of business activity depends primarily on the government's defense-spending program. If that rises, we are told, business activity and prices will rise; but if it declines, there is no telling how much business will deteriorate.

This assumption would lead to the absurd conclusion that the more resources we are forced to devote to making planes, carriers, submarines, nuclear bombs, and guided missiles, the richer we become. Indeed, many amateur economists have not shrunk from this conclusion, and tell us with a knowing air how lucky we are to have a constant threat of Communist aggression—for if this threat were suddenly and miraculously to disappear, what would become of prosperity, "economic growth," and full employment? Every new Communist act of aggression, on this theory, does us an economic favor.

The fallacy consists in looking only at the government's defense payments and forgetting that the money for these comes ultimately from taxes. If defense payments suddenly dropped from $46 billion to $16 billion, taxes could also be cut by $30 billion. Then the taxpayers would have $30 billion more to spend than they had before, to make up for the $30 billion drop in government spending. There is no reason to suppose that the over-all volumes of output or activity would decline.

The whole theory that defense spending is necessary for prosperity, as I pointed out previously, got a crushing refutation at the end of World War II. Immediately after Japan surrendered in August 1945, there was a sweeping cancellation of war contracts. Government economists predicted that unemployment would reach 8 million by the following spring. Nothing of the sort happened.

In sum, there is no reason whatever to suppose even in theory that wages and employment should depend primarily on the volume of defense spending, or government spending for any other purpose. If the government spends $10 billion less on defense *and reduces taxes by the same amount,* then the taxpayers have as much more to spend as the government has less. The total volume of spending is unchanged. It would be a monstrous as well as a foolish doctrine that we must increase the volume of wasteful expenditure on armament, not for the sake of defense, but for the sake of "creating prosperity."

So far as the inflationary effect is concerned, what counts is not the amount of defense spending or total government spending, but the size of the *deficit* and, even more directly, the amount of new money supply. Even the NPA statement at one point seemed willing to settle for a deficit achieved through civilian public works or even a cut in taxes. It even recognized at one point that private plant and equipment modernization might help to create employment. But it paid scant attention to the fact that only the continuing prospect of profits, and only the ability of the profit-earners

65

to retain enough of these from the income-tax collector, can make possible that continued investment of new capital which is essential to put better and better tools in the hands of the workers and constantly to increase their real wages.

What was typical of the NPA statement was that its proposed statist remedies for unemployment utterly ignored the effects of wage rates. No matter how much we are inflating, no matter how high the absolute level of national income or "purchasing power," we can always bring about unemployment by pushing wage rates too high in relation to prices and productivity.

This points to the error in the Keynesian propensity to look only at such huge over-all money aggregates as "national income" and "purchasing power." Maintenance of employment depends on expectation of profits in each industry. This expectation depends on the *relationship* of costs to prices, which means the relationship of prices to each other and wage rates to prices.

21

"Selective" Credit Control

In January 1956, the President's annual Economic Report suggested the restoration of the government's power to regulate the terms of consumer installment credit. The then Secretary of the Treasury, George M. Humphrey, showed political courage as well as excellent sense when he refused to endorse the suggestion.

The Secretary also gave the right reasons why such stand-by powers would be inadvisable. They would put too much discretion in the hands of whoever was to administer them: "You take a great responsibility on yourself when you tell 160 million people what they can afford to buy." Chairman Martin of the Federal Reserve Board also pointed out that: "Selective controls of this nature are at best supplements and not substitutes for the general over-all credit and monetary instruments."

The most eminent advocate at that time of the imposition of stand-by controls on installment credit was Allan Sproul, then president of the Federal Reserve Bank of New York. In a speech on December 29, 1955, he declared: "I do believe that there is a temptation to abuse consumer credit in boom times, that it can thus become a serious source of instability

67

in our economy, and that we would not jeopardize our general freedom from direct controls by giving the Federal Reserve System permanent authority to regulate consumer credit."

But Sproul's argument indirectly admitted that he wished this power in order to avoid a sufficiently firm control over *general* interest rates and the *total volume* of credit: "If there has grown up a form of credit extension which . . . is introducing a dangerous element of instability in our economy, and if it is difficult to reach this credit area by general credit measures without adversely affecting any of the less avid users of credit, is there not a case for a selective credit control?"

What Sproul was saying in effect is that a handful of government monetary managers should be given the power to discriminate among borrowers; to say which are "legitimate" and which not; to say just who should have credit and on what terms. No government body should have such power. It becomes an implement for political favoritism.

President Eisenhower declared in a press conference on February 8, 1956, that if the government were granted stand-by powers over consumer credit they would not be abused. But the record shows that the "selective" powers over credit which already existed had already been abused. Our Federal Reserve authorities complained of "inflationary pressures." Yet at the very time they were suggesting "selective" credit powers they were keeping the official discount rate down to only 2½ per cent. (Within a year and a half they were forced to raise it three times, to 3½ per cent. In that same year—1957—the Bank of England, to stop British inflation, had to raise its discount rate to 7 per cent.) Early in 1956, also, our Federal Reserve authorities had allowed and encouraged a $12 billion increase in the total volume of money and bank credit since the beginning of 1954.

Government authorities discriminate *against* purchase of corporate securities by compelling a minimum down payment of 70 or even 90 per cent. They have discriminated *in favor of* purchase of houses by pledging the taxpayers' money to allow such purchases for a down payment of only 7 per cent or perhaps only 2 per cent. A Congressional subcommittee, in 1956, raised a storm about even these tiny down payments. It asked for a return to the conditions under which a veteran could buy a $10,000 house without putting up even the $200 cash. The belief that government agencies are above the political pressures which lead to such discriminations among borrowers has been disproved everywhere.

In sum, if general interest rates are allowed to rise to their appropriate level, and if there is a sufficiently firm rein on the total quantity of credit, "selective" credit controls are unnecessary. But if there is *not* a sufficiently firm rein on the total quantity of money and credit, "selective" controls are largely futile. If a man has $2,500 cash, for example, but can buy a $10,000 house for only $500 down, then he can also buy a $2,000 car with his "own" cash, whereas if he had to pay down his $2,500 for the house he couldn't buy a car even on pretty loose credit terms. This elementary principle of the shifting or substitution of credit seems to have been overlooked by the champions of "selective" credit controls.

69

22

Must We Ration Credit?

The proposal to restore "selective" or "qualitative" credit controls is revived so often by persons who are regarded as monetary authorities, and is so frequently referred to by them as "one of the necessary weapons to combat inflation," that some further analysis is desirable.

The proposal has the sanction of precedent, for whatever that is worth. Our government used "selective" credit controls at various times between 1941 and 1952. They have been widely imposed in Europe. But the results hardly warrant emulation. Selective credit control is merely one more step along the road toward a command economy. It leads logically back to investment control and to price control.

Selective credit controls are, in fact, government control of short-term investments. The pressure for them comes from special groups of borrowers who want to be favored at the expense of the rest. It comes from monetary managers who lack the courage to refuse such demands; who lack the courage to let general interest rates rise to the point where they will halt inflation. When the price of any commodity is held down by government control, the demand soon exceeds the supply, and the commodity is then rationed. Selective credit controls are merely government rationing of credit.

To ration credit is, of course, to discriminate among would-be borrowers. The decision is thrown into politics and determined by political pressures. This has already happened. Buying a house, even if you can't afford it, is considered so laudable that the taxpayers have been forced to guarantee 95 per cent of the purchase price for you. Buying a refrigerator to put into the house, or a car to get to work from it, is considered much less laudable, so that the terms on which the seller was allowed to extend credit even at his own risk were tightened or "liberalized" by bureaucratic decree. Buying shares in Wall Street (i.e., investing in large-scale industries that increase production and create jobs) is considered so antisocial that the government forbids the seller or the lender to accept less than a down payment of 90 per cent of the full price.

Government "selective" credit decisions are made, in short, on the basis of popular pressures and prejudices. Even if the record were better than this, what are we to say of a system which gives a group of government bureaucrats power to encourage borrowing for one purpose and to discourage it for another; to decide that there should be a boom in industry X but that industry Y should be choked to death? The only reason why "selective" credit controls, here and abroad, have not proved intolerably disruptive is that (for reasons explained in the preceding chapter) such controls seldom achieve their aims.

I shall deal here with only one or two of the many arguments that have recently been put forward in favor of selective credit schemes. It is contended, for example, that "over-all quantitative credit control" is "a pretty crude weapon." The truth is that it would be hard to conceive of a more precise and truly selective instrument for allocating the supply of real savings among credit-worthy borrowers than over-all market interest rates that are allowed to reflect the real conditions of supply and demand. It is nonsense to say that a general rise in interest rates hits only "the little fellow" and favors "the big corporations." One might just as well argue that a general rise in wage rates hits only the little project and helps the big project. Any general rise in costs merely shuts off the marginal projects, regardless of size, that do not seem likely to earn the higher costs.

This is the meaning and function of free markets, in the price of loanable funds as in the price of raw materials and in wages.

23

Money and Goods

Among the popular ideas which make the inflation of our era so hard to combat is the belief that the supply of money ought to be constantly increased "in order to keep pace with the increase in the supply of goods."

This idea, on analysis, turns out to be extremely hazy. How does one equate the supply of money with the supply of goods? How can we measure, for instance, the increase in the total supply of goods and services? By tonnages? Do we add a ton of gold watches to a ton of sand?

We can measure the total supply of goods and services, it is commonly assumed, by values. But all values are expressed in terms of money. If we assume that in any period the supply of goods and services remains unchanged, while the supply of money doubles, then the money value of these goods and services may approximately double. But if we find that the total monetary value of goods and services has doubled during a given period, how can we tell (except by a priori assumption) how much of this is due to an increase of production, and how much to an increase in the money supply? And as the money price (i.e., the "value") of each good is constantly changing in relation to all the rest, how can we measure with exactness the increase of "physical production" in the aggregate?

Yet there are economists who not only think that they can answer such questions, but that they can answer them with great precision. The late Dr. Sumner H. Slichter of Harvard recommended a 2½ per cent annual increase in the money supply in order to counterbalance the price-depressing effect of an assumed annual 2½ per cent increase in "productivity." Dean Arthur Upgren of the Tuck School of Business Administration at Dartmouth wrote in 1955: "Businessmen, bankers, and economists estimate that the nation requires a money supply growth of 4 or 5 per cent a year." He arrived at this remarkable figure by adding "a 1½ per cent a year population growth, a 2½ per cent yearly gain in productivity, and a gain of 1 per cent in the money supply needed to service the more specialized industries." This looked like counting the same thing two or three times over. In any case, it is questionable whether such estimates and calculations, which vary so widely, have any scientific validity.

Yet a lot of people have come to believe sincerely that unless the supply of money can be increased "proportionately" to the supply of goods and services there will not only be a decline in prices, but that this will bring on "deflation" and depression. This idea will not stand analysis.

If the quantity and quality of money remained fixed, and per capita industrial and agricultural productivity showed a constant tendency to rise, there would, it is true, be a tendency for money prices to fall. But it does not at all follow that this would bring about more net unemployment or a depression, for money prices would be falling because real (and money) costs of production were falling. Profit margins would not necessarily be threatened. Total demand would still be sufficient to buy total output at lower prices.

The incentive and guide to production is *relative* profit margins. Relative profit margins depend, not on the absolute level of prices, but on the relationship of different prices to each other and of costs of production (factor prices) to prices of finished goods. An outstanding example of prosperity with falling prices occurred between 1925 and 1929, when full industrial activity was maintained with an average drop in wholesale prices of more than 2 per cent a year.

The idea that the supply of money must be constantly increased to keep pace with an increased supply of goods and services has led to absence of concern in the face of a constant increase in the money supply in the last twelve years. From the end of 1947 to the end of 1959 the supply of bank deposits and currency increased $79 billion, or 46 per cent. And since the end of 1947 average wholesale prices have increased nearly 24 per cent, in spite of an increase in the industrial production index of 60 per cent.

24

The Great Swindle

I present in this chapter a table compiled by the First National City Bank of New York (published in its monthly economic letter of July, 1964) showing the shrinkage in purchasing power of the currencies of 42 countries over the ten-year period 1953-1963. The shrinkage is calculated inversely from the increases in cost-of-living or consumer price index as reported by governments.

It is important to keep this appalling worldwide picture constantly before our minds. It reminds us that inflation is nothing but a great swindle, and that this swindle is practiced in varying degrees, sometimes ignorantly and sometimes cynically, by nearly every government in the world. This swindle erodes the purchasing power of everybody's income and the purchasing power of everybody's savings. It is a concealed tax, and the most vicious of all taxes. It taxes the incomes and savings of the poor by the same percentage as the incomes and savings of the rich. It falls with greatest force precisely on the thrifty, on the aged, on those who cannot protect themselves by speculation or by demanding and getting higher money incomes to compensate for the depreciation of the monetary unit.

Why does this swindle go on? It goes on because governments wish to spend, partly for armaments and in most cases preponderantly for subsidies and handouts to various pressure groups, but lack the courage to tax as much as they spend. It goes on, in other words, because governments wish to buy the votes of some of us while concealing from the rest of us that those votes are being bought with our own money. It goes on because politicians (partly through the second- or third-hand influence of the theories of the late Lord Keynes) think that this is the way, and the only way, to maintain "full employment," the present-day fetish of the self-styled progressives. It goes on because the international gold standard has been abandoned, because the world's currencies are essentially paper currencies, adrift without an anchor, blown about by every political wind, and at the mercy of every bureaucratic caprice. And the very governments that are inflating profess solemnly to be "fighting" inflation. Through cheap-money policies, or the printing press, or both, they increase the supply of money and credit and affect to deplore the inevitable result.

	Indexes of Value of Money			Annual Rates of Depreciation (Compounded)		
	1953	1958	1963	'53-'58	'58-'63	'53-'63
Guatemala	100	95	95	1.0%	...%	0.5%
Ceylon	100	97	93	0.6	0.8	0.7
El Salvador	100	90	92	2.1	—0.4	0.9
Venezuela	100	97	92	0.6	1.2	0.9
United States	100	93	88	1.5	1.2	1.3
Belgium	100	92	87	1.7	1.2	1.4
Canada	100	92	87	1.7	1.2	1.4
Portugal	100	95	86	1.0	1.9	1.5
Pakistan	100	91	86	1.9	1.2	1.5
Ecuador	100	98	85	0.4	2.7	1.6

	Indexes of Value of Money			Annual Rates of Depreciation (Compounded)		
	1953	1958	1963	'53-'58	'58-'63	'53-'63
Switzerland	100	93	84	1.5	2.1	1.8
Germany	100	92	82	1.7	2.2	2.0
South Africa	100	87	82	2.7	1.2	2.0
Philippines	100	95	81	1.0	3.1	2.1
Australia	100	88	81	2.5	1.7	2.2
India	100	91	78	1.9	2.9	2.4
Austria	100	90	78	2.1	2.7	2.4
Ireland	100	86	78	3.0	1.9	2.4
Netherlands	100	85	77	3.2	1.9	2.5
United Kingdom	100	86	77	3.0	2.2	2.6
New Zealand	100	85	77	3.2	2.1	2.6
Italy	100	88	75	2.5	3.1	2.8
Norway	100	85	75	3.2	2.6	2.9
Sweden	100	84	73	3.4	2.7	3.1
Japan	100	92	72	1.7	4.7	3.2
Denmark	100	86	71	3.0	3.8	3.4
Greece	100	76	70	5.3	1.7	3.6
Finland	100	78	67	4.9	3.1	3.9
France	100	83	66	3.7	4.4	4.0
Mexico	100	66	59	8.0	2.1	5.0
Iran	100	72	56	6.4	4.9	5.6
Spain	100	71	55	6.6	4.9	5.7
Israel	100	72	55	6.4	5.1	5.7
Peru	100	74	50	5.8	7.6	6.7
China (Taiwan)	100	68	46	7.4	7.6	7.5
Colombia	100	66	40	8.0	9.4	8.7
Turkey	100	58	38	10.3	8.2	9.3
Uruguay	100	57	18	10.6	20.6	15.8
Argentina	100	46	9	14.4	27.3	21.1
Brazil	100	42	6	15.9	31.9	24.4
Chile	100	13	5	33.5	18.2	26.3
Bolivia	100	4	3	47.5	7.9	30.5

Note: Depreciation computed from unrounded data and measured by reciprocals of official cost-of-living or consumer price indexes.

25

Easy Money=Inflation

In the early summer of 1957, Secretary of the Treasury Humphrey, testifying before a Congressional committee, gave a lucid lesson on the causes of inflation and an impressive answer to the advocates of cheap money.

The inflationists were contending at the time that the Administration had been reducing the volume of credit, and causing "inflation" and higher prices by raising interest rates.

As to the volume of credit, the Secretary had no difficulty in showing that it had actually "expanded substantially in the last four years." "There is more credit outstanding today than ever before." In fact, as the Secretary pointed out, if one counted mortgage, consumer, corporate, and other forms of nonbank credit, the total had *increased* over 1952 by the staggering sum of $146.5 billion ($135.8 billion from "savings" and $10.7 billion "from bank credit expansion, or increased money supply"). The "tight money" complaint, as the Secretary showed, merely reduced itself to this—that the government had put some limits on monetary expansion.

Humphrey gave the best official answer yet made to the frequent contention that an increase in interest rates raises prices because interest rates are a cost of production. On

79

the basis of the gross sales of all manufacturers, he pointed out that of the cost of an article selling for $100, about 33 cents represented (explicit) interest. During the ten-year period since 1946 "prices of goods that consumers buy rose 27½ per cent, or $27.50 on a $100 item [due to labor and other costs], compared with the 20-cent increase due to higher interest."

His comparisons in home-building were no less impressive. A house that cost $10,000 to build in 1946 would cost $19,000 in 1957. If the interest rate on an FHA mortgage increased from 4 per cent in 1946 to 5 per cent in 1957, then the monthly mortgage payment (on the basis of 15 per cent down and a twenty-year amortization) would increase from $51.51 on the 1946 house to $106.58 on the 1957 house. Only $8.71 of this increase would be due to the higher interest cost; the other $46.36 would be due to other costs raised by inflation.

But to hold down interest rates artificially is to encourage borrowing, and thereby to increase the money-and-credit supply. It is this increased money supply that raises prices (and costs) and constitutes the heart of inflation.

The real criticism to be made of the Federal Reserve in 1957 (and still) was not that it had kept credit too scarce and interest rates too high, but that it had yielded to inflationist pressure. It had made credit too plentiful and kept interest rates too low. It is precisely because interest rates were still too low in 1957 that the demand for credit still exceeded the supply. A discount rate of only 3 per cent (when 91-day Treasury bills yielded 3.404 per cent) was inflationary. The Fed might still be well-advised to follow the example of Canada and keep the discount rate always at least ¼ of 1 per cent above the bill rate. Such a course would not be sufficient to halt inflation, but it would be an indispensable condition. It would also have an important political advantage, for it would show that the Fed was merely following the market, and not arbitrarily raising interest rates.

26

Cost-Push Inflation?

Sometime in early 1957 the theory broke out in several places that we are now confronted with a "new" kind of inflation. As described at the time by Robert C. Tyson, chairman of the finance committee of the U.S. Steel Corporation: "Our new kind of inflation appears to be cost inflation pushing prices up, rather than price inflation pulling up costs through competitive bidding for materials and manpower. We might think of it as a new cost-push type as distinquished from the conventional demand-pull type of inflation."

Going even further, a study by the National Industrial Conference Board declared: "Although money supply has been checkreined by Federal Reserve policy, business is still on the uptrend . . . Since prices have continued to rise, the clear lesson of 1956 is that money and its rate of use are not the sole determinants of price . . . Today, the critical question is: How adequate are monetary controls for coping with price pressures that arise from nonmonetary forces?"

Now such theories seem to me to mix truth with error. The Conference Board attempted to prove its case statistically. But as the U.S. Bureau of Labor Statistics pointed out on May 13, 1957, in a study of productivity, costs, and prices: "Where the figures indicate that prices and unit labor costs showed about the same increase, or that one or the other showed a greater increase during a particular year or period of years, this should be taken as a description of what happened and not necessarily as an explanation of what 'caused' the change. An increase in unit labor costs may lead to an increase in price, but conversely an increase in price can result in strong pressure for increases in wages ... The answer to the question of whether the wage increases cause the price increase or vice versa cannot be determined from the figures alone."

The BLS report went on to declare: "Average hourly compensation [of workers] in current dollars increased much more than productivity during the postwar period [1947-56]. The former increased by about 61 per cent, the latter by 26 per cent, leading to an increase in employe compensation per dollar of real product of about 28 per cent."

This sounded ominous, but only because it was confusingly stated. Four paragraphs further down, the report declared: "The increase of about 28 per cent in employe compensation per dollar of real product was almost identical with the increase in price between 1947 and 1956." In other words, the word "productivity" in the first quotation must have meant productivity in *real* terms, not in *dollar-value* terms. Multiply the 26 per cent increase in "productivity" by the 28 per cent increase in price level, and we get the same 61 per cent increase as in hourly labor income.

The Conference Board tried to prove that the increase

in the money supply could not be the cause of the price rise in the preceding two years, because the money supply had not gone up in this period. But this overlooked longer comparisons, and mistakenly assumed that changes in money supply must reflect themselves exactly proportionately in prices with neither time lag nor anticipations. Expansion of the money (and credit) supply is both the necessary and the sufficient cause of inflation. Without such expansion, an excessive increase in wage rates would lead merely to unemployment.

I regret having to criticize what were otherwise two excellent and informative statistical reports. And insofar as they describe *political pressures,* the "cost push" theorists are right. Our politicians put irresponsible and irresistible power in the hands of union leaders, and then plead with them not to use it. They remove the natural economic penalties on recklessness, and then beg for restraint. If the Federal Reserve seriously tried to hold the line on money and credit, while the union leaders kept pushing up wage rates, it is the Federal Reserve, not the unions, that the politicians would blame for the consequent unemployment and recession.

As long as the political climate remains this unhealthy, a halt to inflation is impossible. But with understanding and courage, inflation could be halted overnight.

27

Contradictory Goals

In January of 1957, the Guaranty Trust Company of New York, in its monthly Survey, discussed a problem that had already engaged the attention of leading European economists and was becoming urgent here. This involved the clash in the economic objectives of governments which assume "responsibility" for the achievement of certain "goals."

Since the end of World War II governments everywhere have been pursuing three mutually contradictory aims. These are (1) constantly rising wages, (2) stable prices, and (3) full employment.

It should be obvious that these goals cannot all be achieved at the same time. Even in the short run, any two of these goals can be achieved only at the sacrifice of the third. Thus if we try to have constantly rising wages (regardless of productivity), we can have full employment only if we are willing to allow prices to go up to maintain profit margins, and only if we increase monetary purchasing power enough to enable consumers to pay the higher prices. But this is another way of saying that we must give up the goal of stable prices and encourage a continuous inflation.

If we try to have both constantly rising wages and stable prices, we soon arrive at a point where we can have them only at the cost of unemployment, and eventually of mass unemployment. If we want both stable prices and full employment, then the constant annual "rounds" of wage increases, as a result of strikes or strike threats (and regardless of what has happened to productivity), will have to be abandoned.

However, given the pressures from union leaders and other groups, and given the prevailing obsession that government "must assume responsibility" for everybody's economic welfare, the de facto choice of Western governments in the last decade or two has been constantly rising wages and full employment financed by a so-called "creeping" inflation.

There are not lacking, indeed, rationalizations of this very course, among the most candid of which is that of the late Sumner H. Slichter of Harvard. Professor Slichter seemed to think that a "creeping" inflation of some 2 per cent a year would be both necessary and acceptable. It had already been pointed out by Dr. Winfield Riefler of the Federal Reserve that, even if we assume we could control an inflation to a rate of 2 per cent a year, "it would be equal to an erosion of the purchasing power of the dollar by about one-half in each generation." The legalized robbery that such a "solution" would involve of millions of savings-bank depositors, life-insurance policyholders, bondholders, and of everyone dependent on a fixed or sluggishly responsive income, is itself sufficient ground for rejecting it.

Even so, it would not work. The moment an inflation is

planned, acknowledged, and *foreseen,* the game is up. Inflation is a swindle. You cannot tell your intended victim in advance that you intend to swindle him. Slichter proposed his plan mainly in order to meet annual wage demands. But union leaders, if the plan were put into effect, would simply add 2 per cent (or whatever the planned annual inflation was) on top of the demands they would have made anyway. In fact, lenders, investors, merchants, speculators would all mark up their demands or change their operations to beat the inflation, which, out of control, would race to a crack-up.

What is still understood only by an appallingly small minority even of the "experts" is that prices, in the early stage of an inflation, usually rise by *less* than the increase in the money supply, but in the later stage of an inflation always rise by *more* then the increase in the money supply.

Yet there is one way in which the three goals of rising wages, stable prices, and full employment (when these goals are reasonably interpreted) could all be achieved. This way is through the restoration of a sound currency and a genuinely free economy. In such an economy, it is true, wages could not for long rise faster than marginal labor productivity, but they would rise *as fast as* marginal labor productivity, though the rise in their real purchasing power might be reflected more in lower prices than in higher wage rates.

87

28

"*Administered*" *Inflation*

Gardiner C. Means, an economist who invented the term "administered prices" in the '30s, came up in 1957 with the theory that the current inflation is an "administered" inflation. The solution, he thought, would be for the President to call a conference of business and labor leaders and get an agreement from them to "hold the line" for a year or two on wages and prices.

But his theory of causation was and is false. His proposed remedy was not needed, and is not needed now. It would not work, but would greatly aggravate the very evil it is supposed to cure.

Past inflations, he agrees, have been "monetary" inflations —the result of an increased money supply bidding for the available supply of goods and services. This is correct. And it applies to *every* inflation, including the present one (i.e., 1939 to 1960 to ?).

This can be shown by any set of long-term comparisons. At the end of 1939, the total supply of money and bank credit (total bank deposits plus currency outside of banks) was $64.7 billion. In March of 1957 it was $221.5 billion, an increase of 246 per cent. In 1939 wholesale prices were at an index number of 50.1; in 1957 they were at a level of 117.4, an increase of 136 per cent. The chief reason why wholesale prices did not go up even more in this period is that there was also a great increase in production. The increase in the money supply is a sufficient explanation of the present inflation. We do not have a "new kind" of inflation, and we do not need new explanations.

Neither logic nor statistical comparisons give any support to the "administered price" theory of inflation. If sellers can administer prices to any level they choose, why weren't prices as high in 1957, or in 1955, or 1949, or 1939, or 1914, as they are today? Why have prices all been raised now? What has prevented them from going still higher?

Certain prices, it is true, are administered (within narrow limits) at levels different from those that a perfectly fluid competition would bring about. The outstanding directly administered prices are those administered by government. This includes all public-utility rates and railroad rates. But these are administered down rather than up. Farm prices have of course been supported by government above free-market levels. Farm products in 1957 had risen 150 per cent since 1939, whereas industrial products had risen only 116 per cent.

By far the most important administered price is the price of labor. Money wage rates have been administered upward by powerful industrywide labor unions. Since 1939 hourly wages in manufacturing industries had increased in 1957 by 229 per cent.

As a cure for all this, Means in 1957 would have had the President call a conference of business and labor leaders at

89

which he would "get agreement from them to hold the line" on prices and wages. Now such agreements would be extremely harmful if they were uniformly adhered to. They would not allow for the relative changes in particular prices and wages necessary to adjust output to changes in supply and demand.

All hold-the-line legislation or voluntary agreements in the past have broken down under political pressures, chiefly in favor of wage increases. The Means plan left-handedly recognized this. His proposed agreements would have allowed "small" wage increases to take account of increases in productivity, and increases "where a major disparity in particular wage rates required correction." Anyone who remembers our World War II experience must know that such loopholes would be exploited to the point where the hold-the-line agreements would become a farce. But even this would be better than their strict enforcement; for to try to hold a uniform line on prices and wages, particularly if the money and credit supply continued to be increased, would have a disastrous effect on production.

Schemes of the Means type are wholly unnecessary. All that is needed to stop the present inflation is a halt to the expansion of the money-and-credit supply and repeal of the legislation that creates monster unions and gives them a coercive wage-raising power that employers are impotent to resist.

29

Easy Money Has An End

The maintenance of short-term interest rates at too low a level, by governments or central banks, is one of the main explanations of the continuance of inflation in Europe and in the United States. Excessively low rates always encourage overborrowing, which means an expansion in the supply of money and credit, which in turn causes commodity prices to rise even further.

It is possible, of course, for a government or a central bank to keep money rates low for a long time, either by printing money directly or by permitting the overborrowing and consequent expansion of credit to which excessively low money rates inevitably lead. What is less well understood is that cheap money cannot be continued indefinitely. It sets in motion forces that eventually drive interest rates higher than if a cheap-money policy had never been followed.

The expansion of money and credit that is necessary to hold interest rates down also raises commodity prices and wages. Higher commodity prices and wages make it necessary for businessmen to borrow correspondingly more in order to do the same volume of business. Therefore the demand for credit soon increases as fast as the supply. Later on, still another factor comes in. When both borrowers and lenders begin to fear that inflation is going to *continue,* prices and wages begin to go up *more* than the increase in the supply of money and credit. Borrowers want to borrow still more to take advantage of the expected further rise in prices, and lenders insist on higher interest rates as an insurance premium against expected depreciation in the purchasing power of the money they lend.

When this happens in an extreme degree, we get a situation like that in Germany in November of 1923, when rates for "call money" went up to 30 per cent per *day*. This phenomenon in mild degree became evident in Britain in 1957. When the U.S. Treasury 2½s were trading around 86 in June of 1957, for example, the British Treasury 2½s issued in 1946 could be bought at 50, or half the original purchase price. Yet corporate shares in Britain had been bid up to levels where returns to the investor were in many cases substantially lower than on gilt-edge bonds. As one London investment house explained the matter: "The argument is, indeed, put forward that, since the pound has been depreciating in the past decade at an average rate of 4¾ per cent per annum, any investment likely to show a total net return on income and capital accounts over a given period of less than this amount is giving a negative yield and should be discarded."

The attractions of easy money were coming to an end. That is why, in September 1957, the Bank of England raised its discount rate to 7 per cent.

30

Can Inflation Merely Creep?

As nearly everybody professes to be against inflation (even those who fervently advocate the very things that cause it), it was refreshing to read a writer like the late Sumner H. Slichter of Harvard, who frankly accepted inflation as a "necessary evil" and did not think we could prosper without it.

He was careful, it is true, to say that he was only in favor of "creeping" inflation, not galloping inflation, though he was often vague concerning the exact point where a creep became a canter. He was at times indiscreet enough to suggest that a price rise of 2 or 3 per cent a year would be about right. It has been pointed out, however, that even if we could control an inflation to a rate of 2 per cent a year it would mean an erosion of the purchasing power of the dollar by about one-half in each generation.

Even so, this would not accomplish Slichter's announced purpose. He thought prices must go up this much in order to meet the unions' annual wage demands. But the moment Slichter's inflation scheme was openly put into effect, as I have already pointed out in Chapter 27, union leaders would simply add 2 per cent (or whatever the planned annual inflation was) on top of the demands they would have made anyway. In fact, lenders, investors, manufacturers, retailers, speculators would all mark up their demands or change their operations to beat the inflation, which would thereupon race to a crack-up. A declining currency must eventually obey the law of acceleration that applies to all falling bodies.

In the *Harvard Business Review* of September-October, 1957, Slichter not only continued to commend a creeping inflation, but reprimanded Neil H. Jacoby, a former member of the Council of Economic Advisers, and C. Canby Balderston, vice chairman of the Board of Governors of the Federal Reserve System, for being against inflation. Without going into a detailed analysis of all the confusions in Slichter's article, it may be helpful to cite a few examples.

He declared that it was "incorrect" to believe that "creeping inflation is bound sooner or later to become galloping inflation," because this had not happened in the preceding twenty-five years in the United States. Yet our cost of living had more than doubled in the preceding seventeen years, which was something more than a creep. Slichter might have taken a look at the French franc, which was then already at considerably less than one-hundredth of its 1914 purchasing power; or at the median loss of one-third of their value by 42 different currencies in the preceding nine years alone (as pointed out in Chapter 24).

Slichter seemed to me to take a somewhat callous attitude about the losses suffered in recent years by the thrifty. Of the millions of savings-bank depositors and holders of government bonds who had seen the purchasing power of their holdings shrink by a third or a half, he wrote coolly: "These people have paid the penalty for poor investment judgment." Their poor judgment consisted, in brief, in trusting their country's money and in answering their government's appeal to buy war bonds.

Slichter's proposals were based on his obsessive idea that constant creeping inflation was necessary to maintain full employment. This led him to misstate an argument of Jacoby's as a "suggestion that prices be kept stable by permitting unemployment to fall below 4 per cent." The truth is that full employment or its absence has no necessary connection whatever with inflation, but depends wholly upon the maintenance of fluid and functional interrelationships between wage rates and prices and profits. Slichter did not seem to understand the argument that unions cannot raise the real wages of the whole body of workers, and his attempted refutation missed the point.

Finally, in his efforts to minimize the harm done by inflation, Slichter failed to see that when employment is reasonably full, further inflation must hurt on net balance as many people as it helps, for the gains in dollar income resulting from inflation must be offset by the losses in dollar purchasing power.

31

How to Wipe Out Debt

When it was pointed out to the Eisenhower Administration, as it was to its Democratic predecessors, that our huge national debt continues to mount, a favorite defense was that it had not risen as a percentage of the national income.

Such a reply ignores the fact that the national income has gone up (in dollar terms) in large part because prices have gone up, and that prices have gone up because of the currency debasement brought about partly by the very deficit financing that increased the debt. What this defense amounts to, in short, is a boast that the burden of the national debt has not increased because it can now be paid off in debased dollars.

There are few governments today that cannot make such a boast. At the end of this chapter is a table, taken from the August 1957 issue of *Pick's World Currency Report,* showing what happened in the preceding nine years to the national public debts of a dozen leading countries. Only three of them were smaller in terms of their own currencies; the other nine were all larger in terms of their own currencies. Yet in spite of the fact that they owed more in nominal currency units than a decade previously, the United States, Brazil, France, Sweden, and the United Kingdom owed much less in real terms than a decade previously. Though the U.S. debt increased 24 billion in dollars since 1948, the reduced purchasing power of the dollar wiped out the equivalent of $42 billion of that debt. Though France increased its debt since 1948 from 3,412 billion to 6,506 billion francs, it also wiped out 3,383 billion francs of the 1948 purchasing power of such a debt.

This is the way governments are today cheating their creditors—precisely the citizens who responded to their patriotic appeals for help.

There is nothing new about this process. It was old when Adam Smith denounced it in "The Wealth of Nations" in 1776: "When national debts have once been accumulated to a certain degree, there is scarce, I believe, a single instance of their having been fairly and completely paid. The liberation of the public revenue, if it has ever been brought about at all, has always been brought about by a bankruptcy; sometimes by an avowed one, but always by a real one, though frequently by a pretended payment.

"The raising of the denomination of the coin has been the most usual expedient by which a real public bankruptcy has been disguised under the appearance of a pretended payment. . . . A pretended payment of this kind . . . extends the calamity to a great number of other innocent people. . . . When it becomes necessary for a state to declare itself bankrupt, in the same manner as when it becomes necessary for an individual to do so, a fair, open, and avowed bankruptcy is always the measure which is both least dishonorable to the debtor, and least hurtful to the creditor. The honor of a state is surely very poorly provided for, when, in order to

97

cover the disgrace of a real bankruptcy, it has recourse to a juggling trick of this kind, so easily seen through, and at the same time so extremely pernicious."

Adam Smith then goes on to show how "almost all states . . . ancient as well as modern" have "played this very juggling trick." It may be added that, since the substitution of paper for metallic money, the trick has become much easier and therefore more frequent. It may also be added that the debtor class today, including as it does most corporation stockholders, is probably as rich as the creditor class, which includes savings-bank depositors and owners of savings bonds.

NATIONAL DEBTS
(In billions of currency units)

	1948	1957	1957
			Adjusted to 1948
		Nominal	*Power*
		Paper Units	*Purchasing*
United States $	252	276	234
Canada $	15	14	10
Argentina p.	18	95	26
Belgium fr.	245	328	279
Brazil cr.	23	67	20
France fr.	3,412	6,506	3,123
Italy l.	2,315	4,805	3,604
Netherlands fl.	26	18	12
Spain p.	53	90	59
Sweden kr.	11	14	10
Switzerland fr.	11	8	7
United Kingdom £	25	27	18

32

The Cost-Price Squeeze

From time to time during the present inflation (let's say between 1940 and 1964) violent disputes have broken out concerning who or what caused it. "Labor" and "management" blame each other.

Attacks on management have frequently come from Walter Reuther, head of the United Automobile Workers. In 1957, for example, Reuther contended that "exorbitant" profits, not wages, had been the villain promoting inflation. Otis Brubaker, research director of the steelworkers' union, declared at the same time: "Wage increases have not caused a single price increase in twenty years."

These charges provoked replies. In its letter of October 1957, the First National City Bank of New York pointed out: "Regardless of what year is taken as a base [from 1939 on] wages and total employment costs in the steel industry have far outstripped gains in productivity. Measuring from 1940, the gain in productivity of 56 per cent, while substantial, fell far short of increases in hourly earnings and total employment costs amounting to more than 200 per cent. The result . . . was an approximate doubling of unit labor costs with inevitable pressure for higher prices."

A much wider study of the same problem was published by the National Association of Manufacturers in September of the same year. It found that the history of manufacturing since the end of World War II had been one of rising costs per unit of output—particularly labor costs and taxes. Compensation of employes rose 23 per cent per unit of output between 1948 and 1956. Corporate taxes rose 32 per cent on the same basis. But prices of manufactured goods rose only 10 per cent. The result was a reduction of 25 per cent in profit per unit of output between 1948 and 1956.

The decline in the profit margin of manufacturing industries was particularly striking when expressed as a percentage of sales. It dropped from 4.9 per cent in 1948 to 3.1 per cent in 1956. (By way of comparison, the figure for 1929 was 6.4 per cent; for 1937, 4.7 per cent; for 1940, 5.5 per cent.) Thus, concluded the NAM study, "between 1948 and 1956 profit margins as a per cent of sales have fallen from a level characteristic of prosperity years to a level characteristic of recession years." Higher costs cannot automatically be recouped by higher market prices.

These statistical comparisons by the National City Bank and the NAM proved that the inflation was at least not the result of the "greed" of manufacturers for exorbitant profits, as Reuther contended. But they did not prove that "the conclusion is inescapable," as the NAM study put it, "that the current inflationary push is due to the rising costs of labor and the continuing heavy tax burden."

The rise in wages, it is true, as both studies pointed out, exceeded the rise in "productivity." But the studies compared *money* wages to *physical* output. In any inflation, no matter how caused, money wages are practically certain to rise more than physical productivity. This is simply because both wages and prices rise in every inflation. It does not necessarily follow that the rise in prices has been *caused* by the rise in wages. Both may have risen from a common cause.

That common cause is not hard to find. Neither the wage rise nor the price rise since 1939 or 1948 would have been possible if it had not been fed by an increased money supply. The money-and-credit supply (total bank deposits plus currency) increased from $64.7 billion at the end of 1939, to $172.7 billion at the end of 1948, to $226.4 billion at the end of 1956, to $313.8 billion at the end of 1963. There would have been no inflation, in short, in the last ten or twenty years without the cooperation and connivance of the monetary authorities.

This does not mean, of course, that union pressure has had no responsibility for the result. Under present labor laws the government has not merely encouraged but in effect forced the creation of industrywide unions with power to impose continuous wage increases. Unless these excessive union powers are reduced, they must either lead to unemployment by forcing costs above prices, or create political pressure for still more monetary inflation.

33

The Employment Act of 1946

Under a gold standard the primary objective of a nation's monetary policy was clear: It was to protect the integrity of the currency by maintaining gold convertibility at all times. Under a paper standard and a Keynesian ideology the objectives become confused. The U.S. Employment Act of 1946 declares that "it is the continuing policy and responsibility of the Federal government to use all practicable means . . . to promote maximum employment, production, and purchasing power." Many interpret this as a standing order for inflation. Chairman Martin of the Federal Reserve Board has suggested that Congress should declare "resolutely—so that all the world will know—that stabilization of the cost of living is a primary aim of Federal economic policy."

An infinitely better solution would be simply repeal of the Employment Act of 1946. But if that mischievous law is kept, it should at least be amended to add the requirement of price stability as an offset to the heavy inflationary bias in the law as it now stands.

It is not inherently desirable to make price stability an

official goal of government policy. It implies a further extension of statism. But this is the kind of awkward problem we create when we abandon a gold standard.

34

Inflate? Or Adjust?

In the midst not only of moderate but even of the wildest inflations, there are sudden breaks, slumps, or lulls. Whenever these occur, the inflationists declare that the inflation has ended and that we are now facing recession or deflation unless we immediately adopt their "stabilizing" measures. Such a slump occurred in the late months of 1957 and the early months of 1958. Though wholesale and consumer prices continued to rise, interest rates, industrial production, and employment declined. The proposed remedies started to pour in.

To those of us who had lived through the Great Depression, there was a curious familiarity about these schemes. On June 12, 1931, for example, the Chase National Bank of New York published a pamphlet by its economist, the late Benjamin M. Anderson, called "Equilibrium Creates Purchasing Power." Anderson there drew a contrast between two opposing schools of thought. The school to which he adhered found the cause of the slump in "a disturbance of economic equilibrium." The other found its causes in "deficiencies of purchasing power."

The purchasing-power school was inflationist. It advocated "cheap-money policies," farm price supports, and heavy spending on "public works." It argued that "reductions in wages are on no account to be permitted." "The general picture which the purchasing-power school presents is that of production running ahead of buying power." As against this, Anderson advocated the restoration of equilibrium, mainly through adjustments of free and flexible prices and wages. He called for the restoration of a proper balance among the various types of production, among prices, and particularly between prices and costs of production, including wages, so that profits would be possible and the prospect of them would once more stimulate enterprise.

"When goods are produced in proper proportions," he wrote, "they clear the markets of one another. . . . Production itself gives rise to the income which supports consumption. Production and consumption expand together. The 120 millions of people in the United States consume vastly more than the 400 millions in China, because they produce vastly more. . . . The problem is merely one of keeping the different kinds of production in proper proportion. This is accomplished under the capitalist system by the movement of prices and costs. Labor and capital tend to get out of lines where return is low and to move over into lines where return is better. The smooth working of this system calls for flexible prices, competitively worked out, which tell the truth regarding underlying supply and demand conditions."

Anderson went on to point out that the purchasing-power theory was not working. "We have had extremely cheap money for over a year." Inflexibility of industrial wage-rates, while prices were falling, had led to increased unemployment. "Real" industrial wage-rates between June 1929 and March 1931 had risen 11 per cent, indirectly helping to force down "real" farm wages 17 per cent.

However, as we know, the purchasing-power school—the inflationist school—won out. We had cheap money, inflexible or rising wage rates, and heavy government deficits for the next ten years. As a result, we also had mass unemployment for the next ten years—until World War II finally bailed us out.

Today the chief ideological change is that there can hardly be said to be two schools of thought. Practically everyone in Washington seems to agree that we can easily float ourselves out of slumps through more inflation. We need merely give ourselves a sufficiently big dose—of increased spending, or tax reduction, or anything else that will produce a whopping deficit. The new bible is Keynes's "General Theory," which denies Say's Law and ignores any need for specific wage and price adjustments. In early 1958, the Republican Administration disagreed with the Democratic inflationists only about the question of timing. It hoped (justifiably, as it turned out) everything would cure itself in the next few months. If it didn't, it promised to take "positive government action"—today's euphemism for more inflation.

Meanwhile, neither political party called attention to the fact that as factory wage-rates had risen, unemployment had increased and payrolls had fallen. Neither party asks today whether even massive inflation can restore employment as long as powerful unions have escalator contracts under which wage-rates soar faster than living costs, preventing restoration of profit margins or lowering of prices. The only remedy proposed is bigger and longer unemployment compensation to help strong unions preserve upward-spiraling wage-rates.

35

Deficits vs. Jobs

I pointed out in the last chapter that, after 1930, we had cheap money, inflexible or rising wage-rates, and heavy government deficits for the next ten years. As a result, we also had mass unemployment for the next ten years—until World War II finally bailed us out.

Inasmuch as today, in every slump or lull, we are being urged to adopt precisely the remedies that failed in the '30s, it may pay us to look at that period in more detail. The deficits, number of unemployed, and percentage of unemployed to the total labor force are tabulated, year by year, in that decade.

	Deficit (billions of dollars)	Unemployed (millions)	Percentage of Unemployment
1931	$0.5	8.0	15.9
1932	2.7	12.1	23.6
1933	2.6	12.8	24.9
1934	3.6	11.3	21.7
1935	2.8	10.6	20.1
1936	4.4	9.0	16.9
1937	2.8	7.7	14.3
1938	1.2	10.4	19.0
1939	3.9	9.5	17.2
1940	3.9	8.1	14.6

In the tabulation the deficits are for fiscal years ending on June 30; the unemployment is an average of the full calendar year. Spenders, no doubt, will try to find a partial negative correlation between the size of the deficit and the number of unemployed; but the central and decisive fact is that heavy deficits were accompanied by mass unemployment. If we translate the figures into 1959 terms, we find: The average deficit in this ten-year period was $2.8 billion, which was 3.6 per cent of the gross national product of the period. The same percentage of the gross national product of 1959 would mean a deficit of $17.3 billion. The average unemployment of the ten-year period was 9.9 millions, which was 18.6 per cent of the total labor force. The same percentage of unemployment today would mean 13.4 million jobless. So much for the effect of deficits as a cure for unemployment.

At the end of this chapter the table is continued from 1941 through 1963. It will be noticed that we did, in 1944, get unemployment down to a low point of only 1.2 per cent of the working force. If this is to be attributed to deficit spending, then we must notice that it took a $51.4 billion deficit to do it. Compared with the increase in the gross national product, this would have to be a deficit today of more than $145 billion! (However, the deficits in both 1943 and 1945 were even larger than in 1944; and yet unemployment was also larger in those years.)

Another point to be noticed in this table is that in the ten years from 1948 to 1957 inclusive, average unemployment was 4.3 per cent of the total labor force. Yet this period was one of unusually high employment, even of "labor shortage." But if four persons out of every 100 are "normally" unemployed, "abnormal" unemployment is only the excess above this. Such unemployment is serious, especially for those directly concerned. But it hardly justifies reckless deficit spending or further dilution of the dollar in an effort to cure it. We could more profitably look, in times of abnormal unemployment, at the relation of key wage rates to prices and consumer demand.

THE RECORD

	Employed	Unemployed	Percentage of
	(in millions)		Unemployment
1941 ················	50.4	5.6	9.9%
1942 ················	53.8	2.7	4.7
1943 ················	54.5	1.1	1.9
1944 ················	54.0	.7	1.2
1945 ················	52.8	1.0	1.9
1946 ················	55.3	2.3	3.9
1947 ················	57.8	2.4	3.9
1948 ················	59.1	2.3	3.8
1949 ················	58.4	3.7	5.9
1950 ················	59.7	3.4	5.3
1951 ················	60.8	2.1	3.3
1952 ················	61.0	1.9	3.1
1953 ················	61.9	1.9	2.9
1954 ················	60.9	3.6	5.6
1955 ················	62.9	2.9	4.4
1956 ················	64.7	2.8	4.2
1957 ················	65.0	2.9	4.3
1958 ················	64.0	4.7	6.8
1959 ················	65.6	3.8	5.5
1960 ················	66.7	3.9	5.6
1961 ················	66.8	4.8	6.7
1962 ················	68.0	4.0	5.6
1963 ················	68.8	4.1	5.7

36

Why Cheap Money Fails

The late Lord Keynes preached two great remedies for unemployment. One was deficit financing. The other was artificially cheap money brought about by central bank policy. Both alleged remedies have since been assiduously pursued by nearly all governments. The result has been worldwide inflation and a constantly shrinking purchasing power of monetary units. But the success in curing unemployment has been much more doubtful. In the last chapter we considered the unpromising results of budget deficits. Does cheap money have any better record?

On the next page is a table covering the twelve years from 1929 through 1940, comparing the average annual rate of prime commercial paper maturing in four to six months with the percentage of unemployment in the same year. Both sets of figures are from official sources.

In sum, over this period of a dozen years low interest rates did *not* eliminate unemployment. On the contrary, unemployment actually *increased* in years when interest rates went down. Even in the seven-year period from 1934 through 1940, when the cheap-money policy was pushed to an average infra-low rate below 1 per cent (0.77 of 1 per

Year	Commercial Paper Rate	Percentage of Unemployment
1929	5.85%	3.2%
1930	3.59	8.7
1931	2.64	15.9
1932	2.73	23.6
1933	1.73	24.9
1934	1.02	21.7
1935	0.75	20.1
1936	0.75	16.9
1937	0.94	14.3
1938	0.81	19.0
1939	0.59	17.2
1940	0.56	14.6

cent), an average of more than seventeen in every hundred persons in the labor force were unemployed.

Let us skip over the war years when war demands, massive deficits, and massive inflation combined to bring overemployment, and take up the record again for the last eleven years (table on next page).

It will be noticed that, although the commercial paper interest rate in this period averaged 2.48 per cent—more than three times as high as that in the seven years from 1934 through 1940,—the rate of unemployment was not higher, but much lower, averaging only 4.4 per cent compared with 17.7 per cent in the 1934-40 period.

Within this second period, the relationship of unemployment to interest rates is almost the exact opposite of that suggested by Keynesian theory. In 1949, 1950, and 1954, when the commercial paper interest rate averaged about 1½

Year	Commercial Paper Rate	Percentage of Unemployment
1949	1.49%	5.5%
1950	1.45	5.0
1951	2.16	3.0
1952	2.33	2.7
1953	2.52	2.5
1954	1.58	5.0
1955	2.18	4.0
1956	3.31	3.8
1957	3.81	4.3 *
1958	2.46	6.8
1959	3.97	5.5

* Unemployment percentages before 1957 are based on Department of Commerce "old definitions" of unemployment; for 1957 and after they are based on the "new definitions," which make unemployment slightly higher—4.2 per cent of the labor force in 1956, for example, instead of the 3.8 per cent in the table.

per cent, unemployment averaged 5 per cent and more. In 1956, 1957, and 1959, when commercial paper rates were at their highest average level of the period at 3.70 per cent, unemployment averaged only 4.4 per cent of the working force.

In brief, neither deficit spending nor cheap-money policies are enough by themselves to eliminate even prolonged mass unemployment, let alone to prevent unemployment altogether.

The only real cure for unemployment is precisely the one that the Keynesians and inflationists reject—the adjustment of wage rates to the marginal labor productivity or "equilibrium" level—the balance and co-ordination of wages

113

and prices. When wage rates are in equilibrium with prices, there will tend to be full employment regardless of whether interest rates are "high" or "low." But regardless of how low interest rates are pushed, there will be unemployment if wage rates are too high to permit workable profit margins.

37

How to Control Credit

Within a period of ten days, in 1958, the Federal Reserve authorities illustrated first the wrong and then the right way to control inflation. On August 4 they raised the margin requirements for buying stock from 50 to 70 per cent. (On October 16 they raised them again to 90 per cent.) On August 14 they permitted the Federal Reserve Bank of San Francisco to raise its discount rate from 1¾ to 2 per cent. The first method is what is called "selective" credit control. The second is what is called general credit control. Only the second is equitable and effective.

The targets of selective credit controls are always politically selected. The stock market is the No. 1 target because those with no understanding of its role and function in the American economy regard it as a sort of glorified gambling casino. As G. Keith Funston, president of the New York Stock Exchange, said in a speech in October 1957:

"I sometimes wonder at our sense of proportion. A man can borrow up to 75 per cent to buy a car, 100 per cent to buy a washing machine, and 94 per cent to buy a house. But he can borrow only 30 per cent to buy an interest in the company that makes the car, the washing machine, or the house.

We have made it much easier to borrow in order to spend, than to borrow in order to save."

In addition to being discriminatory, these rigid restrictions on stock-buying margins are also in the long run futile. We cannot encourage a *general* inflationary flood and then expect to dam off its effects in one direction. Credit, like water, seeks its level and leaks through every crack. If a man is determined to buy shares, and does not have the required legal margin, he can mortgage his house or other assets and use the proceeds in the stock market.

Raising stock-market margin requirements seldom has the intended effects. No statistics can show, of course, what *might* have happened to stock-market credit or prices if margins had *not* been changed. But most margin increases have shown little effect on stock-market credit.

Nor is it easy to justify the 1958 rise of margin requirements on this ground. As Funston then pointed out, customers' net debit balances on June 30, 1958 (when margin requirements were 50 per cent), totaled $3.1 billion, which represented only 1.4 per cent of the market value of all stocks listed on the New York Stock Exchange on the same date, a ratio almost exactly the same as it was a month earlier or a year before.

Increases in margin requirements have sometimes temporarily halted the upward movement of stock prices, but never for more than a month or two. In fact, in every instance of a margin increase from February 1945 through April 1955, stock prices six months later averaged at least 12 per cent higher than in the six months before the margin change. The average price of stocks in October 1958, when the 90 per cent margin requirement was put into effect, was 54.55 on the Standard-and-Poor index; in the following July, with that margin requirement still in effect, it had risen to an average of 59.74.

This is what we might have expected. The price that people pay for stocks is primarily determined by the expected yield from those stocks and the capitalization of that yield as affected by interest rates.

However, because the increases in legal stock margin requirements have not had their *intended* effect, it does not follow that they have done no harm. Their main effect, careful comparisons show, has been to *reduce the volume of trading*—sometimes as much as 25 per cent. This does not merely mean that brokers lose commissions. It reduces the liquidity of the market and throws a damper on the willingness and ability of corporations to raise new money through stock issues.

38

Who Makes Inflation?

Over the last quarter century the American government has displayed a peculiarly schizophrenic attitude toward spending vs. economy, inflation vs. dollar-integrity.

This has been frequently reflected in the annual Economic Report of the President. A good example is the Economic Report of President Eisenhower transmitted to Congress on January 20, 1959. "An indispensable condition for achieving vigorous and continuing economic growth," he wrote, "is firm confidence that the value of the dollar will be reasonably stable in the years ahead." But most of the report endorsed policies that tended to undermine this confidence.

Describing governmental actions that helped "to bring about a prompt and sound recovery" the President declared: "Monetary and credit policies were employed vigorously to assure ample supplies of credit. Legislation was enacted to lengthen temporarily the period of entitlement to unemployment benefits. Numerous actions were taken to spur building activity. Steps were taken to accelerate Federal construction projects already under way and to speed up projects supported by Federal financial assistance. Activities under a number of Federal credit programs, in addition to those in the housing field, helped counter the recession. And the acceleration of defense procurement . . . exerted an expansive effect."

Every one of these policies was inflationary. All of them meant pouring new money and credit into the system, increasing the supply of dollars, reducing their individual purchasing power. In a later part of the report it was admitted that the Federal Reserve policies enabled the commercial banks "to add nearly $10 billion in loans and investments to their assets" in 1958, largely by "additions to their holdings of U.S. Government securities." This in turn added $13.6 billion to the total money supply (including inflated time deposits), and helped to boost living costs.

Yet the President's report blurred responsibility for inflation and tried to shift it on to consumers, business, and labor. The "individual consumer" was advised to "shop carefully for price and quality"—as if he couldn't be depended upon to do that without urging. The government in effect was saying to consumers: "Here are $10 billion or more additional paper dollars; but don't be reckless enough to spend them, because it will make *you* responsible for raising prices." "Businessmen" were told they "must wage a ceaseless war against costs"—as if self-interest and self-preservation did not ensure that. But nothing was said about Federal labor laws (including compulsory exclusive "bargaining") which rendered the employer all but impotent in resisting excessive demands. And "leaders of labor unions" (after having been granted monopolistic bargaining powers by law) were urged not to ask as much as they could get under these conditions. This meant that they would not last very long as labor leaders.

The President went on to declare: "If the desired results cannot be achieved under our arrangements for determining wages and prices, the alternatives are either inflation, which would damage our economy and work hardships on millions of Americans, or controls, which are alien to our traditional way of life and which would be an obstacle to the nation's economic growth and improvement." What the President seemed to be saying is that it was consumers, businessmen, and labor leaders who threatened to bring inflation by lack of "self-discipline and restraint," and that they might "force" government controls.

But the real culprit was and is government. Government must stop deficit spending, stop flooding the country with more paper dollars, and stop encouraging monopoly in the labor field while blaming "our free competitive economy" for rising wages and prices.

Perhaps the most important recommendation in the Economic Report of January 1959 was that Congress "amend the Employment Act of 1946 to make reasonable price stability an explicit goal of Federal economic policy, coordinate with the goals of maximum production, employment, and purchasing power now specified in that act." If the mischievous Employment Act of 1946 is to be retained, such an amendment on net balance would probably make it less mischievous, because the act has been constantly interpreted as a directive to inflate. But an immensely better solution would be to repeal the act altogether.

39

Inflation As a Policy

In his classic little history of fiat money inflation in the French Revolution, Andrew D. White points out that the more evident the evil consequences of inflation became, the more rabid became the demands for still more inflation to cure them. Today, as inflation increases, apologists emerge to suggest that, after all, inflation may be a very good thing—or, if an evil, at least a necessary evil.

Until recently, the chief spokesman of this group was the late Prof. Sumner H. Slichter of Harvard. I should like to discuss here what I consider to be three of his chief wrong assumptions: (1) That a "creeping" inflation of 2 per cent a year would do more good than harm; (2) that it is possible for the government to *plan* a "creeping" inflation of 2 per cent a year (or of any other fixed rate); and (3) that inflation is necessary to attain "full employment" and "economic growth."

We have already noticed, in Chapter 30, that even if the government could control an inflation to a rate of "only" 2 per cent a year, it would mean an erosion of the purchasing power of the dollar by about one-half in each generation. This could not fail to discourage thrift, to produce injustice, and to misdirect production. Actually inflation in the United States has been much faster. The cost of living has more than doubled in the last twenty years. This is at a compounded rate of about 4 per cent a year.

The moment a *planned* "creeping" inflation is announced or generally expected in advance, it must accelerate into a gallop. If lenders expect a 2 or 4 per cent rise of prices a year, they will insist that this be added to the interest rate otherwise paid to them to maintain the purchasing power of their investment. If borrowers also expect such a price rise, they will be willing to pay such a premium. All businesses, in fact, will be forced to offer a correspondingly increased gross rate of return to attract new investment, even new equity capital. If there is a planned price rise, union leaders will simply add the expected amount of that rise on top of whatever wage demands they would have made anyway. Speculators and ordinary buyers will try to anticipate any planned price rise—and thereby inevitably accelerate it beyond the planned percentage. Inflation forces everybody to be a gambler.

The burden of Slichter's argument was that "a slow rise in the price level is an inescapable cost of the maximum rate of growth"—in other words, that inflation is a necessary cost of "full employment." This is not true. What is necessary for maximum "growth" (i.e., optimum employment and maximum production) is a proper relationship or *coordination* of prices and wages. If some wage-rates get too high for this coordination, the result is unemployment. The cure is to correct the culpable wage-rates. To attempt to lift the whole level of prices by monetary inflation will simply create new maladjustments everywhere.

In brief, if a real coordination of wages and prices exists, inflation is unnecessary; and if coordination of wages and prices does not exist—if wages outrace prices and production—inflation is worse than futile.

Slichter assumed that there is no way to restrain excessive union demands except by "breaking up" unions. Yet we need merely repeal the special immunities and privileges conferred on union leaders since 1932, especially those in the Norris-La Guardia and Wagner-Taft-Hartley acts. If employers were not legally *compelled* to "bargain" with (in practice, to make concessions to) a specified union, no matter how unreasonable its demands; if employers were free to discharge strikers and peaceably to hire replacements, and if mass picketing and violence were really prohibited, the natural competitive checks on excessive wage demands would once more come into play.

40

The Open Conspiracy

More than thirty years ago—in 1928, to be precise— H. G. Wells published a minor propagandistic novel called "The Open Conspiracy." Though I reviewed it at the time, I've forgotten now exactly what that open conspiracy was. But the description seems to fit with peculiar aptness something that is happening in the United States today. Our politicians, and most of our commentators, seem to be engaged in an open conspiracy not to pay the national debt—certainly not in dollars of the same purchasing power that were borrowed, and apparently not even in dollars of the present purchasing power.

There is of course no explicit avowal of this intention. The conspiracy is, rather, a conspiracy of silence. Very few of us even mention the problem of substantially reducing the national debt. The most that even the conservatives dare to ask for is that we stop piling up deficits so that we do not have to increase the debt and raise the debt ceiling still further. But anyone with a serious intention of eventually paying off the national debt would have to advocate over-balancing the budget, year in, year out, by a sizable annual sum.

Today one never sees nor hears a serious discussion of this problem. We see hundreds of articles and hear hundreds of speeches in which we are told how we can or should increase Federal expenditures or Federal tax revenues in proportion to the increase in our "gross national product." But I have yet to see an article that discusses how we could begin and increase an annual repayment of the debt in proportion to the increase in our gross national product.

When we look at the dimensions the problem has now assumed, it is not difficult to understand the somber silence about it. If someone were to propose that the debt be paid off at an annual rate of $1 billion a year, he would have to face the fact that at that rate it would take 289 years, or nearly three centuries, to get rid of it. Yet $1 billion a year is even now no trivial sum. Republican Administrations, after World War I, did succeed in maintaining something close to such a steady annual rate of reduction between 1919 and 1930; but they were under continual fire for such a "deflationary" policy. Because of such deflationary fears, one would hardly dare mention a higher rate today.

One suspects that there is at the back of the minds of many of the politicians and commentators who sense the dimensions of the problem an unavowed belief or wish. This is that a continuance of inflation will scale down the real burden of the debt in relation to the national income by a constant shrinkage in the value of the dollar, so reducing the problem to "manageable proportions." Such a policy would be indignantly disavowed. But this is precisely what our reckless spending is leading to. On the debt we contracted twenty years ago we are paying interest and principal in 48-cent dollars. Are our politicians hoping to swindle government creditors by paying them off in dollars twenty years from now at less than half the purchasing power of the dollar today?

This trick, alas, has a long and inglorious history. I hope I may be forgiven for repeating here part of the quotation from Adam Smith's "Wealth of Nations" that I made in Chapter 31. "When national debts have once been accumulated to a certain degree," wrote Smith in 1776, "there is scarce, I believe, a single instance of their having been fairly and completely paid. The liberation of the public revenue, if it has been brought about at all, has always been brought about by a bankruptcy; sometimes by an avowed one, but always by a real one, though frequently by a pretended payment [i.e., payment in an inflated or depreciated monetary unit]. . . . The honor of a state is surely very poorly provided for, when, in order to cover the disgrace of a real bankruptcy, it has recourse to a juggling trick of this kind, so easily seen through, and at the same time so extremely pernicious."

Our government is not forced to resort, once more, to such a "juggling trick." It is not too late for it to face its responsibilities now, and to adopt a long-term program that would eventually pay off its creditors with at least the present 48-cent dollar, without plunging us further into inflation or deflation.

41

How the Spiral Spins

For years we have been talking about the inflationary wage-price spiral. But Washington (by which is meant both the majority in Congress and officials in the Administration) talks about it for the most part as if it were some dreadful visitation from without, some uncontrollable act of nature, rather than something brought about by its own policies.

Let us see just how those policies, over the last twenty-five years, have produced the wage-price spiral. First of all, under a series of laws beginning most notably with the Norris-La Guardia Act of 1932, followed by the Wagner Act and by its later modification, the Taft-Hartley Act, we decided that labor troubles developed chiefly because there was not enough unionization and because unions were not strong enough.

Therefore we in effect put the Federal government into the union-organizing business. We compelled employers to deal exclusively with the unions thus quasi-officially set up, regardless of how unreasonable the demands of these unions might turn out to be. Though illegalizing all efforts to deny employment to workers who joined unions, we explicitly legalized arrangements to deny employment to workers who did not join unions.

But worst of all, we gave to the unions and union members a privilege not granted to any other associations or individuals—the power of private coercion and intimidation. By the Norris-La Guardia Act we in effect prevented either employers or non-union employes from going to the Federal courts for immediate relief from irreparable injury. We refuse, contrary to legal practice in every other field, to hold a union liable for the acts of its agents. We tolerate mass picketing, which is intimidating and coercive, preventing employers from offering to other workers the jobs abandoned by strikers, and preventing other workers from applying for such jobs. And then we are astonished and indignant when these special privileges, against which we provide no effective legal protection, are "abused."

The inevitable result of these laws is that we have built up huge unions with the power to bring basic national industries to a halt overnight. And when they have done this, we can think of no way of getting an industry started again except by giving in to the demands of the union leaders who have called the strike.

This accounts for the upward push on money wage-rates. But it does not account for the inflationary spiral. The effect of pushing wage-rates above the level of marginal labor productivity, taken by itself, would simply be to create unemployment. But as F. A. Hayek has put it: "Since it has become the generally accepted doctrine that it is the duty of the monetary authorities to provide enough credit to secure full employment, whatever the wage level, and this duty has in fact been imposed upon the monetary authorities by statute, the power of the unions to push up money wages cannot but lead to continuous, progressive inflation."

Soon or late our Federal lawmakers and administrators must face up to the labor-union-boss dictatorship and the wage-price spiral that their own laws and actions have created. But they refuse to do this when each new crisis arises. When, for example, a nationwide steel strike is prolonged, they become panicky. They seek to settle it by the only means that seem possible to them—by giving in once more to union demands, by granting still another wage increase and setting off a new upward wage-price spiral.

Politicians demand that the President appoint a "fact-finding" board to "recommend," i.e., to impose, in effect, compulsory arbitration that would compel the employers to grant another increase to employes. Thus one government intervention begets a further government intervention. Because government has failed in its primary task—that of preventing private coercion—politicians ask, in effect, for price and wage fixing; and we are driven toward totalitarian controls.

42

Inflation vs. Morality

Inflation never affects everybody simultaneously and equally. It begins at a specific point, with a specific group. When the government puts more money into circulation, it may do so by paying defense contractors, or by increasing subsidies to farmers or social security benefits to special groups. The incomes of those who receive this money go up first. Those who begin spending the money first buy at the old level of prices. But their additional buying begins to force up prices. Those whose money incomes have not been raised are forced to pay higher prices than before; the purchasing power of their incomes has been reduced. Eventually, through the play of economic forces, their own money-incomes may be increased. But if these incomes are increased either less or later than the average prices of what they buy, they will never fully make up the loss they suffered from the inflation.

Inflation, in brief, essentially involves a redistribution of real incomes. Those who benefit by it do so, and must do so, at the expense of others. The total losses through inflation offset the total gains. This creates class or group divisions, in which the victims resent the profiteers from inflation, and in which even the moderate gainers from inflation envy the bigger gainers. There is general recognition that the new distribution of income and wealth that goes on during an inflation is not the result of merit, effort, or productiveness, but of luck, speculation, or political favoritism. It was in the tremendous German inflation of 1923 that the seeds of Nazism were sown.

An inflation tends to demoralize those who gain by it even more than those who lose by it. The gainers become used to an "unearned increment." They want to keep their relative gains. Those who have made money from speculation prefer to continue this way of making money instead of working for it. I remember once, early in 1929, a conversation between two friends, both of whom held prominent posts as book reviewers but both of whom were heavily in the stock market. They were exchanging stories about their profits. "Today your salary," they agreed, "is just a tip." People do not like to work full time just for a tip. The long-term trend in an inflation is toward less work and production, and more speculation and gambling.

The profiteers from inflation tend to spend freely, frivolously, and ostentatiously. This increases the resentment of those who have been less favored. The incentive to ordinary saving, in the form of savings accounts, insurance, bonds, or other fixed-income obligations, tends to disappear. The spectacle of quick and easy returns increases the temptations to corruption and crime.

It is not merely that inflation breeds the gambling spirit and corruption and dishonesty in a nation. Inflation is itself an immoral act on the part of government. When modern governments inflate by increasing the paper-money supply, directly or indirectly, they do in principle what kings once did when they clipped the coins. Diluting the money supply with paper is the moral equivalent of diluting the milk supply with water. Notwithstanding all the pious pretenses of governments that inflation is some evil visitation from without, inflation is practically always the result of deliberate governmental policy.

This was recognized in 1776 by Adam Smith in "The Wealth of Nations." Though I have quoted the passage before, it bears repeating: "When national debts have once been accumulated to a certain degree, there is scarce, I believe, a single instance of their having been fairly and completely paid. The liberation of the public revenue, if it has ever been brought about at all, has always been brought about by a bankruptcy; sometimes by an avowed one, but always by a real one, though frequently by a pretended payment."

The pretended payment was inflation. The U.S. government today is paying off in 48-cent dollars the debts it contracted in 1940. Adam Smith went on: "The honor of a state is surely very poorly provided for, when, in order to cover the disgrace of a real bankruptcy, it has recourse to a juggling trick of this kind, so easily seen through, and at the same time so extremely pernicious."

43

How Can You Beat Inflation?

From time to time I get letters from readers asking how they can protect themselves from the eroding effects of inflation on their savings. Many pamphlets from investment advisers attempt to tell people how this can be done. Schemes are constantly proposed for the issuance of government bonds and other securities with interest payments or redemption values that would increase in the same proportion as the cost of living. Many other schemes are put forward to counter the bad effects of inflation.

Both the advice and the schemes indirectly call attention to one of the worst results of inflation. It steadily wipes out the value of dollar savings, of savings-bank deposits, of bonds, of mortgages, of insurance benefits, of pensions, of fixed-income payments of every kind. It thereby penalizes and discourages thrift and saving, discourages the "safer" and more conservative investments, and forces everybody to be a speculator or gambler. For if, in the midst of an inflation, a man leaves his money in savings banks or mortgages or fixed-interest securities, he faces a certain loss in its real purchasing power.

Can any scheme be devised that would offset this effect?

133

The escalator clauses in wage contracts are an attempt to do this for union labor. Proposals are frequently made that private companies, or the government itself, should issue bonds on which the interest payments, as well as the redemption value at maturity, would increase by the same percentage as the official index of consumer prices.

But the objections to such schemes are very serious. The borrower, whether a private company or the government, would assume an obligation of unknown extent. It would have no assurance, particularly if the subsequent inflation were severe, that its own income would rise proportionately to the cost of living (or, to put the matter another way, in inverse proportion to the drop in the value of the dollar). Such "escalator" bonds, like the escalator wage contracts, would simply increase the number of people with no interest in halting the ravages of inflation against the rest of the population.

What is not understood by those who propose these schemes is that inflation can benefit one group only at the expense of other groups. The price of what you have to sell can go up more or faster than the average price of what you have to buy only if the price of what *other* people have to sell to you goes up less or slower than the price of what *they* have to buy from you. The net amount of any real gain from inflation must be offset by an equivalent amount of real loss. Roughly speaking, one half of the population can gain from inflation only at the expense of the other half. The political appeal of inflation comes from fostering the illusion in the great majority of voters that they will somehow get the better of the swindle, and profit at the expense of a few unidentified victims.

If we grant that it would be possible to devise any scheme by which the gains from inflation would exactly equal the losses, so that nobody would either gain or lose by it, then all the arguments which sustain inflation would collapse. For inflation does not come without cause. It is the result of policy. It is the result of something that is always within the control of government—the supply of money and bank credit. An inflation is initiated or continued in the belief that it will benefit debtors at the expense of creditors, or exporters at the expense of importers, or workers at the expense of employers, or farmers at the expense of city dwellers, or the old at the expense of the young, or this generation at the expense of the next. But what is certain is that everybody cannot get rich at the expense of everybody else. There is no magic in paper money.

It is true that an alert individual can do certain things to protect himself from the eroding effects of inflation on the value of his dollars—but only on the assumption that he acts both sooner and more wisely than the majority.

Even this used to be easier than it is today. In the German inflation which culminated in 1923, for example, a German could always buy American dollars, at whatever the current rate happened to be, as soon as his monthly, weekly, or daily income above current needs became available to him. But as German internal prices went up much slower than the dollar (or, more accurately, as the external value of the German mark fell much faster than its internal value), even this proved an inadequate "hedge" for the German people considered as a whole. As the rush to buy foreign currencies made the external value of the mark depreciate even faster (so that, at the end, it took hundreds of billions of them to buy a single dollar), there was no profit in the operation for the latecomers.

Today, Americans have no completely safe major foreign currency to turn to to protect them against further depreciation of their own dollar. They are prohibited by law from buying and holding gold at home. (This is a left-handed confession by our monetary authorities that the people do prefer gold to paper and would make the exchange if they could.) If they buy gold abroad, they face the risk that our government (following the domestic precedent of 1933), may force them to turn in their gold holdings at an arbitrary value in paper dollars.

They are left, then, in practice, with the choice of buying real estate, common stocks, mink coats and motor cars, television sets and oriental rugs, jewelry—any equity or luxury that is not dollars or a fixed obligation payable in dollars. They are forced, in short, into extravagance and speculation.

An inexpert speculator may, of course, turn to investment trusts or mutual funds which diversify his investment for him and protect him to some extent against his own lack of expert knowledge. But always, the individuals who buy first, or at lower prices, can profit or protect themselves only at the expense of those who buy later or at the top.

It is impossible, in short, for everybody to protect himself against inflation. The early minority can do so only at the expense of the majority, or the early buyers at the expense of the later. And the scramble to get out of money and into things only intensifies the inflation, only increases and accelerates the rise of prices or the fall of the dollar.

This last result must follow whether individuals try to protect themselves against inflation by individual action, or whether they try to do so through such group devices as escalator wage clauses or escalator bond clauses. Even the arithmetic of such schemes is against them. Neither prices nor wages go up uniformly. Suppose some wages and prices do not go up at all, and others go up 100 per cent. The average increase, say, is 50 per cent. Suppose cost-of-living escalator clauses are prevalent, and that wages or prices that have gone up less than 50 per cent are raised to that average. This raises the average increase itself. It may now be 75 per cent. If the prices or wages that have advanced less than this are now raised 75 per cent above the old level, the *average* advance has again been pushed up to, say, 85 per cent. And so on. The process could be stopped only if the monetary authorities refused to supply the added money and credit necessary to sustain successive increases.

There is only one solution—only one sure hedge against inflation that can protect everybody: Don't have the inflation. If you have it, halt it as soon as possible.

44

The ABC of Inflation

Suppose that, by a miracle, every family in the United States were to wake up one morning to find four times as much money in its pockets and its bank account as on the night before. Every family would then be eager to rush out and buy things it had previously longed for and gone without. The firstcomers might be able to buy things at the old prices. But the latercomers would bid prices up against each other. Merchants, with their stocks going down, would reorder, raising wholesale prices. Manufacturers and other producers, because they were doing a bigger business, would try to increase their labor force. This would force up wages. Eventually there would be an increase of prices and wages all around the circle.

This picture is, of course, a violent simplification. But it describes what has actually happened in this country, not overnight, but over the last twenty years or so. At the end of 1939 the amount of currency outside of banks was $6.4 billion. The amount of bank deposits subject to withdrawal by check (which is the main part of the "money supply" with which Americans do business) was $29.8 billion. This made a total active money supply of a little more than $36 billion. At the end of 1967 this money supply had grown to five times as much—$182 billion.

With this hugely increased supply of money bidding for goods, wholesale prices at the end of 1967 had increased 151 per cent above those at the end of 1939. In the same period the cost of living, as measured by the retail prices paid by consumers, had increased 144 per cent. In other words, the purchasing power of the dollar had fallen to only 40 per cent of what it was in 1939.

When we consider the extent of this increase in the money supply, it is surprising that prices have not risen even further. One reason why they haven't is that the supply of goods in the meanwhile has also been increased. Industrial production at the end of 1967 was running at a rate of about 326 per cent greater than in 1939. While the supply of money has quintupled, the rate of output of industrial goods has more than quadrupled.

Let us try to see what inflation is, what it does, and what its continuance may mean to us.

"Inflation" is not a scientific term. It is very loosely used, not only by most of us in ordinary conversation, but even by many professional economists. It is used with at least four different meanings:

1. Any increase at all in the supply of money (and credit).

2. An increase in the supply of money that outruns the increase in the supply of goods.

3. An increase in the average level of *prices*.

4. Any prosperity or boom.

Let us here use the word in a sense that can be widely

understood and at the same time cause a minimum of intellectual confusion. This seems to me to be meaning 2.

Inflation is an increase in the supply of money that outruns the increase in the supply of goods.

There are some technical objections to this (as indicated in Chapter 23), but there are even more serious objections to any of the other three senses. Meaning 1, for example, is precise, but runs counter to all common usage. Meanings 3 and 4, though they do conform with common usage, lead, as we shall see, to serious confusion.

Whenever the supply of money increases faster than the supply of goods, prices go up. This is practically inevitable. Whatever the quantity of anything whatever increases, the value of any single unit of it falls. If this year's wheat crop is twice as great as last year's, the price of a bushel of wheat drops violently compared with last year. Similarly, the more the money supply increases, the more the purchasing power of a single unit declines. In Great Britain, for example, the supply of money increased some 226 per cent between 1937 and the end of 1957; at the same time the cost of living increased 166 per cent. In France, the money supply increased about thirty-six times between 1937 and the end of 1957; the cost of living in France, in the same period, went up about twenty-six times.

The rise of prices, which is merely a *consequence* of the inflation, is commonly talked of as if it were *itself* the inflation. This mistaken identification leads many people to overlook the real cause of the inflation—the increase in the money supply—and to think that the inflation can he halted by the imposition of government price-and-wage controls, even while the supply of money continues to increase. Under such conditions, however, government price-and-wage fixing only discourages, distorts, and disrupts production, *without* curing the inflation.

It is sometimes thought that it is "war" that is responsible for all inflations. But a great part of the present inflations in France, Italy, Great Britain, and the United States have occurred *since* the end of World War II. The American cost of living, for example, has gone up 86 per cent since 1945. And some of the most spectacular recent inflations have occurred in countries relatively untouched by the war. Between 1950 and the end of 1959, the money supply in Chile increased nineteen times, and the cost of living there increased twenty times. In Bolivia, between 1950 and 1959, the money supply was increased seventy times, and the cost of living there increased a hundred times. Similar records could be cited for other countries.

Thus we see that the connection between the increase in the supply of money and the rise in prices is extremely close. All the great inflations of earlier and modern times have been primarily the result of reckless deficit financing on the part of governments, which wanted to spend far more than they had the courage or ability to collect in taxes. They paid for the difference by printing paper money.

Most present-day governments are ashamed to pay their bills directly by printing money, so they have developed more sophisticated and roundabout ways of doing the same thing. Typically, they "sell" their interest-bearing securities to the central bank. The central bank then creates a "deposit" in their favor for the face value of the government

141

securities, and the government draws checks against this "deposit." But all this leads in the end to the same result as printing new money directly.

We are often told, however, that we have in America today a "new" kind of inflation, caused by labor unions forcing constant wage increases. This contention contains a political truth but is misleading economically.

Suppose that unions were able to force up their wage-rates, but that the management of currency and bank credit were such that there was no increase in the total money supply. Then the higher wage-rates would either wipe out profit margins, or they would force manufacturers to raise prices to preserve profit margins. If the higher wage-rates wiped out employers' profits, they would lead directly to unemployment. If they forced a rise in prices, and if consumers had no more money to spend than before, consumers would buy fewer goods. The result would be smaller sales and hence less production and less employment.

An increase in wage-rates, in short, without at least a compensating increase in the money supply, would simply lead to unemployment. But very few governments have the courage to sit tight on the money supply and get the blame for the resulting unemployment. They prefer, instead, to try to make the constantly higher wage-rates payable by constantly increasing the money supply. In this way the rise in wage-rates has *politically* led to the continuance of many inflations.

But there is more than one reason why inflation, in spite

of all the righteous lip-indignation it calls forth, is not only tolerated by the majority of us over long periods, but actively supported by special pressure groups.

The first of these reasons is "the money illusion." We are so accustomed to measuring our incomes and our economic welfare in purely monetary terms that we cannot break ourselves of the habit. Since 1939 the cost of living in the United States has a little more than doubled. This means that a man whose income after taxes has gone up from $5,000 in 1939 to $10,000 now is no better off, in the things he can buy with his income, than he was in 1939.

He is, in fact, definitely worse off. A study by the National Industrial Conference Board, allowing not only for higher prices but for the higher income-tax bite in the later year, estimated that a man required a gross income of $12,307 in 1960 in order to enjoy a purchasing power equal to that of $5,000 in 1939. His gross money-income had to increase still more as he got into the higher income-tax brackets. It took a gross income of $26,030 in 1960 to give him a purchasing power equal to that of $10,000 in 1939 and a gross income of $77,415 to give him a purchasing power equal to that of $25,000 in 1939.

A man whose dollar-income has risen from $5,000 in 1939 to only $7,500 today, after taxes, is definitely worse off. Yet so strong and persistent is the money illusion that millions of people who are worse off in terms of the real purchasing power of their incomes probably imagine themselves to be better off because their dollar income is so much higher.

The money illusion will often be found together with what we may call the special-case illusion. This is the belief that the reason my own money-income has gone up in the last five, ten, or twenty years is that I have been personally very lucky or very talented, whereas the reason the prices I have to pay have gone up is just "inflation." I do not understand the inflation process, however, until I understand that the same forces which have pushed up the prices of what other people have to sell (including their labor services) have pushed up the price of what I personally have to sell. Looking at the matter from the other side, the same general forces which have raised my own income have also raised other people's incomes.

Yet the special-case illusion is not *entirely* an illusion. Here we come to one of the main reasons for the political pressure behind inflation. At the beginning we imagined inflation occurring as the result of a simultaneous miracle by which every family awakened to find its money supply quadrupled overnight. Of course no such miracle happens in real life. No actual inflation happens by a simultaneous or proportional increase in everybody's money supply or money income. No actual inflation affects every person and every price equally and at the same time. On the contrary, every inflation affects different persons and different prices *unequally* and at *different* times.

A typical war inflation, for example, starts when the government uses newly created money to pay armament contractors. First, the profits of the armament contractors increase. Next, they employ more workers, and they raise the wages they pay in order to get and hold more workers. Next, the tradespeople that cater to the armament company owners and employes increase *their* sales. And so on, in widening circles.

In the same way, in a "pump-priming" inflation, brought about by a great public works program or housing program, the first group to benefit are the construction companies, the second the construction workers, the third the tradespeople and others who directly cater to the construction workers— and so on.

Inflation always benefits some groups of the population before it benefits other groups, and more than it benefits other groups. And in most cases it benefits these first groups *at the direct expense* of the other groups.

Suppose, to make an extreme simplification, that one-half of the population has its dollar-income and the prices of its goods or services doubled, while the other half still retains the same dollar-income and can only get the same dollar-prices for its goods. The average prices received by the first half will go from 100 to 200. The average prices received by the second half will remain at 100. This means that the average price of *all* goods will now be 150, or 50 per cent higher than before. The first half of the population will then be about a third better off than before, though not twice as well off, even though its dollar-income has doubled. The second half of the population, though its dollar-income has remained the same, will be able to buy only two-thirds as much goods and services.

In any actual inflation, of course, the relative gains and losses will not be thus neatly split between just two distinct halves of the population; they will vary with every group and even, to some extent, with every family. Yet it will remain true that the losers from an inflation will probably be about equal in numbers to the gainers, even though the money illusion hides this from many of the losers.

The fact that there are always those who can relatively profit from an inflation, while it is going on, even though they do it at the expense of the rest of the community, helps to keep up the political pressure for the continuance of inflation.

The losers from an inflation, if they could always identify themselves and make themselves heard, could more than offset in their political strength the forces that temporarily profit from inflation.

Who are the losers? It is customary to identify them as savings bank depositors, holders of government bonds, elderly retired people or widows living on fixed pensions, insurance-policy holders, teachers and similar white-collar workers. The losers from inflation do include all of these, but they include many more.

Have you personally profited from inflation, or are you one of its victims?

Here is a simple way to find out. In the table on page 147, the second column is based on the U.S. Government's Consumer Price Index. For simplicity of calculation this figure has been converted to a base of 100 for the year 1939. The third column is based on the government's estimate of the per capita "disposable" income (i.e., income after deduction for taxes) in each year. This also has been converted to a base of 100 for the year 1939.

The first thing you want to find out is whether you are

better or worse off *absolutely* than in some earlier year. Put down what your take-home pay was in any chosen past year in the table, add two zeros to it, and divide by the cost-of-living figure for that year. Then take your present take-home pay, add two zeros, and divide the result by the last figure in the column.

If your present income (so recalculated) is greater than

		1939 average = 100
Year	Cost of Living *	Per Capita $ Income **
1939 100		100
1944 127		197
1945 130		200
1946 140		209
1947 161		218
1948 173		238
1949 171		234
1950 173		253
1951 187		272
1952 191		281
1953 193		291
1954 193		291
1955 193		304
1956 196		318
1957 202		326
1958 208		339
1959 210		352
1960 213		361
1961 215		369
1962 218		384
1963 220		396

* Source: U.S. Government Consumer Price Index, as converted from 1957-59 base.

** Source: U.S. Government estimate of per capita disposable personal income in dollars. From table on p. 227, Economic Report of the President, January, 1964. Converted to 1939 base.

your income so recalculated from the past year, then your *real* income has increased. Otherwise you have lost.

Let us take an illustration. Your take-home pay in 1963 say, was $5,000 a year. In 1939 it was $2,500. As you both multiply and divide your 1939 income by 100, it remains at the same figure—$2,500. But you multiply, say, your 1963 income by 100 and divide by 210. This leaves you with only $2,270 of "real" income (i.e., in 1939 dollars) in 1963. Your income in terms of what it would buy, therefore, was lower than it was in 1939.

Suppose, now, you are interested in knowing not only whether you are better or worse off now than in some preceding year in what you can buy with your income, but whether you have done better or worse than the average American in the same period. In a progressive economy like ours, not only total production, and hence total real income, but per-capita production and hence per-capita real income, tend to increase year by year, as capital investment increases and machinery and techniques improve. But the income of some persons has increased much more than that of others. This is partly because, either through ability or good fortune, they hold better positions than formerly; but it may also be because inflation typically benefits some groups at the expense of other groups. As you will notice, unless your dollar income over the last two decades has increased *more* than enough to compensate merely for the increase in living costs in the period, you have not shared proportionately in the increase in the nations real output.

If you wish to get a closer idea of how you made out relatively to others, you can make the same sort of recalculation of your income in the third column as you made in the second. In this recalculation, however, you would have to take more factors into account (such as full family income, after taxes, relative number of persons in the family in the years compared, etc.). And just how much the operations of inflation can be held responsible for whatever the comparison turns out to be, it is impossible to say without a full knowledge of each individual case. But many a person who thinks he has been one of the special beneficiaries of inflation may sharply revise his ideas after such a calculation.

We have still to look at the strongest reason of all why inflation has such powerful political appeal. This is the conviction that it is necessary to maintain "full employment."

Under special conditions inflation can, it is true, have this effect. If, following a boom, maladjustments of various kinds have caused a collapse of demand and of prices, while labor union leaders have refused to accept any compensating cuts in wage-rates, there will of course be unemployment. In such a case a new dose of inflation may raise monetary purchasing power to a point where the old volume of goods will once more be bought at the old price level, and employment may then be restored at the old money-wage level.

But the restoration of full employment could have been brought about just as well if the powerful unions had merely accepted the necessary wage-rate reductions. This would have involved no real sacrifice, because, as prices had collapsed, the cut in wage-rates would merely need to have been great enough to keep the same relative *real* wage-rates (i.e., wage-rates in terms of purchasing-power) as before. Nor, to restore full employment under such conditions, would it be necessary to put into effect any *general* or *uniform* cut in wage-rates. Only those wage-rates would have to be cut that had got out of equilibrium and were causing log-jams in the economy.

Moreover, even if we inject greater and greater doses of monetary inflation, and union demands are such that wage-rates continue to run ahead of prices, then though we will certainly have inflation and higher prices, we will not cure the unemployment.

If we continue to try to solve our difficulties by continued fresh doses of monetary inflation, what will be the upshot? Prices will certainly rise further. But this rise of prices will not guarantee the restoration of full employment. The latter, as we have seen, depends on a generally balanced economic situation, and particularly on the proper relationship between prices and wage-rates.

A serious or long-continued inflation is always in danger of getting out of control. Those who naïvely imagine that our monetary managers, or any other group, know any formula by which we could maintain a predetermined "creeping inflation," with prices rising just 2 or 3 per cent a year, are entirely mistaken. Even if it were not extremely difficult to control exactly the supply of money and credit, there is no assurance whatever that a given percentage of expansion of the money supply from year to year will bring a merely proportional price rise each year. On the contrary, the very knowledge of the existence of such a planned inflation would undermine confidence in the value of the dollar.

It would bring a racing inflation immediately that could quickly get out of hand.

Whenever any inflation gets beyond a critical point (which can never be known in advance), the social losses and evils it brings about are certain to cancel and exceed any initial gains. Holders of bonds or savings deposits at last become aware that the capital value of their savings is shrinking all the time in terms of what it will buy. This awareness discourages thrift and savings. The whole structure of production becomes distorted. Businessmen and corporations are deceived by the way inflation falsifies their books. Their inventory profits are illusory. Their depreciation deductions are inadequate. It becomes impossible for business managers to know to what extent their paper profits are real. But these profits often *look* bigger and bigger on paper. They provoke charges of "profiteering." Demagogues use them to inflame class hatreds against business.

Inflation makes it possible for some people to get rich by speculation and windfall instead of by hard work. It rewards gambling and penalizes thrift. It conceals and encourages waste and inefficiency in production. It finally tends to demoralize the whole community. It promotes speculation, gambling, squandering, luxury, envy, resentment, discontent, corruption, crime, and increasing drift toward more intervention which may end in dictatorship.

How long will inflation continue? How far will it go?

No one has a sure answer to such questions. The answer is in the hands of the American people. Yet inflation is not necessary and it is never inevitable. The choice between chaos and stability is still ours to make.

Index of Names

FUNK & WAGNALLS PAPERBOOKS

The Aldus Shakespeare

FUNK & WAGNALLS PAPERBOOKS